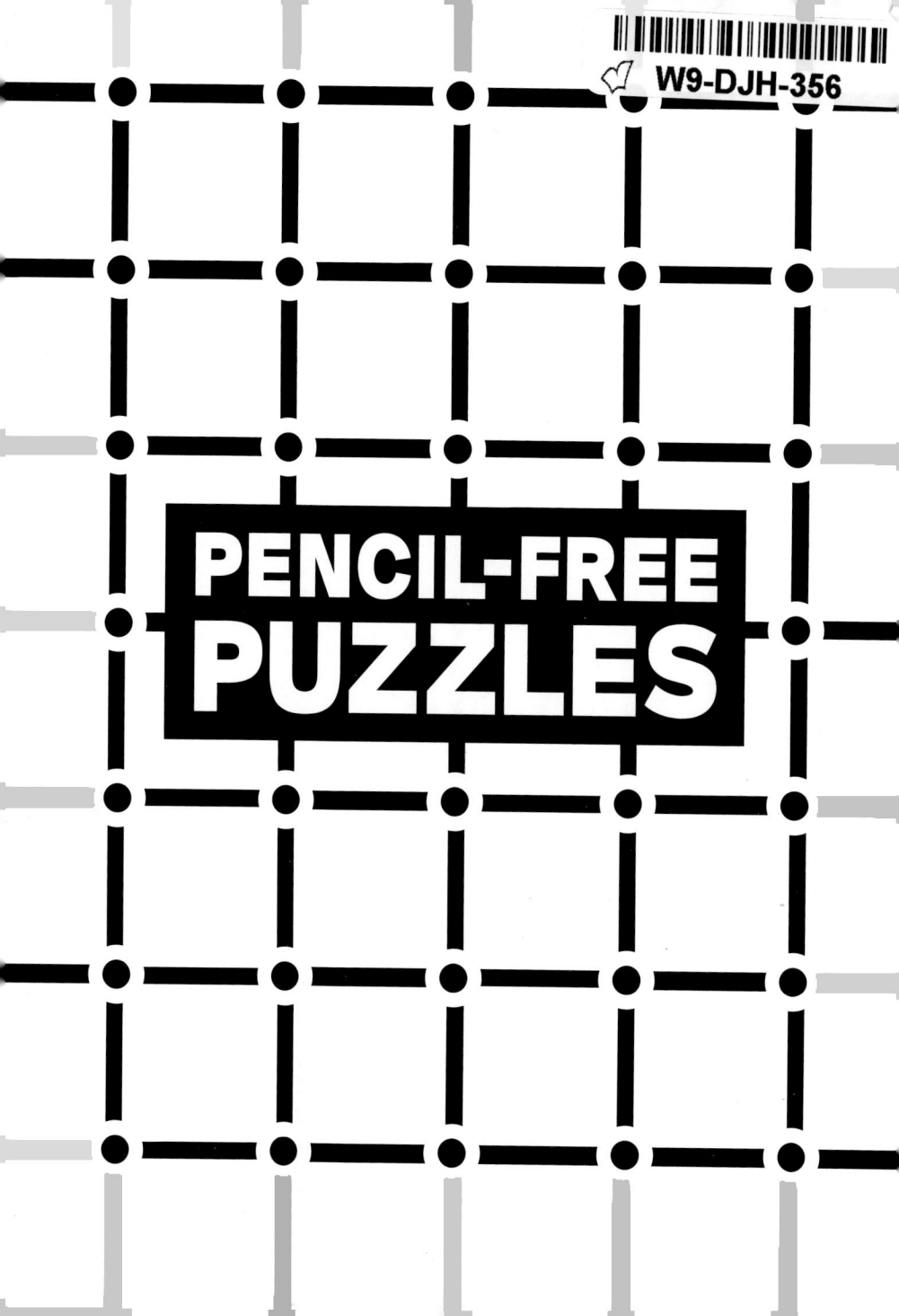

PENCIL-FREE PUZZLES

Inspiring | Educating | Creating | Entertaining

Brimming with creative inspiration, how-to projects, and useful information to enrich your everyday life, Quarto Knows is a favorite destination for those pursuing their interests and passions. Visit our site and dig deeper with our books into your area of interest: Quarto Creates, Quarto Cooks, Quarto Homes, Quarto Lives, Quarto Drives, Quarto Explores, Quarto Gifts, or Quarto Kids.

© 2020 Quarto Publishing Group USA Inc.
Text © 2004 by Nathan Haselbauer

First Published in 2020 by Fair Winds Press, an imprint of The Quarto Group, 100 Cummings Center, Suite 265-D, Beverly, MA 01915, USA. T (978) 282-9590 F (978) 283-2742 QuartoKnows.com

Fair Winds Press titles are also available at discount for retail, wholesale, promotional, and bulk purchase. For details, contact the Special Sales Manager by email at specialsales@quarto.com or by mail at The Quarto Group, Attn: Special Sales Manager, 100 Cummings Center, Suite 265-D, Beverly, MA 01915, USA.

24 23 22 21 20   1 2 3 4 5

ISBN: 978-1-59233-977-8

Digital edition published in 2020

Library of Congress Cataloging-in-Publication Data available

Cover Design: Landers Miller Design
Interior Illustration and Layout: Landers Miller Design

Printed in China

Contents

This book contains a rich selection of 190 brainteasers—from math and logic problems to word games. All of them are extremely short—you should be able to solve most of them in your head in just a minute or two! You won't need an advanced mathematical background to figure them out. All you need is an active intelligence and an inquisitive mind. You'll find the answers at the back of the book— but don't look! So put on your thinking cap, get started, and some have brainteasin' fun!

THE PUZZLES

01

When Peter and Bill ran a 100-meter race, Peter won by five meters. To give Bill a chance to win, they raced again, but this time Peter started five meters behind the starting line.

Each man ran the race at the same speed as in the first race.

What were the results of the second race?

02

Billy bought a pack of baseball cards and found a rookie card worth 10.00. He decided to sell it to his friend Tommy for 10.00. After the baseball season ended, the card was worth more and Billy bought it back from Tommy for 15.00. The following year, Billy sold the card for 8.00. Did Billy make or lose money in the end?

03

A teacher told her students, "I have a bag of lollipops that I bought for 6.25. Can anyone figure out how many are in the bag and how much I paid for each one?" The students looked puzzled and said there's no way anyone could know how many lollipops were in the bag.

The teacher said, "The lollipops were all the same price. The number I bought is the same as the number of cents each cost." Can you figure out how much the lollipops cost?

04

Tricia, Kelly, Sasha, and Meredith started a book club that will meet once a month. Each month, one person hosts the party and another person brings the snacks. The host gets to pick the book and one of the other three has to bring the snacks. The responsibility of the host and the provider of snacks changes every month. How many months will it take until there has been every possible combination of host and snack-provider?

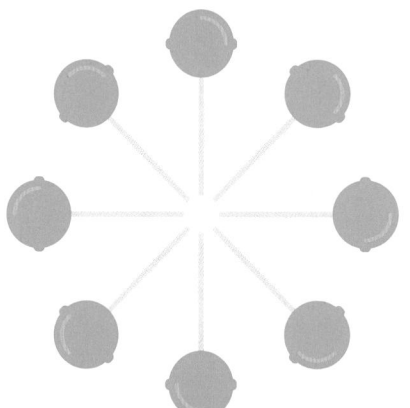

05

The Washington Metro system buys wheels for their rail cars for 200 per wheel. The wheels last for ten years and then they have a scrap value of 25 apiece. If rust-proofing treatment costing 50 a wheel is applied, each wheel will last fifteen years but will have no scrap value. In the long run, would it be more cost effective to rust-proof the wheels or not?

06

Ian and Adam wanted to go to Coney Island and were trying to figure out the fastest way to get there. Ian wanted to take the subway, but Adam noted that the subway only gets halfway to Coney Island and then you have to walk the rest of the way. Adam said the fastest way to get there would be by bicycle, but Ian still felt the subway would be faster. So Adam hopped on his bicycle and Ian took the subway. The subway was four times as fast as Adam on his bicycle, but Adam was twice as fast as Ian's walking speed. Who got to Coney Island first?

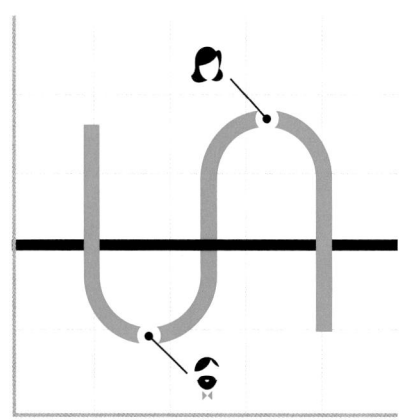

07

After graduating from college, Alison went to work for a financial firm and Eric went to work for a law firm, both earning the same amount. Last year, Alison had a raise of ten percent and Eric had a drop in pay of ten percent. This year, Alison had a ten percent drop in pay and Eric had the ten percent raise. Who is making more now, or are they getting paid the same?

08

Both Aaron and Alexander are average marksmen and only hit their target fifty percent of the time. They decide to fight a duel in which they exchange alternate shots until one is hit. What are the odds that the man who shoots first will hit the other?

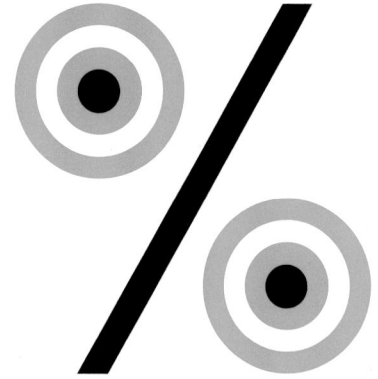

09

If Beth is as old as Bill will be when Trish is as old as Beth is now, who is the oldest?

10

A rowboat is floating in a swimming pool. Will dropping a marble in the pool or in the rowboat raise the level of the water in the pool higher?

11

Patti and John decided to play squash against each other, betting 10.00 on each game they played. Patti won three games and John won 50.00. How many games did they play?

12

On a digital clock, how many times in the first twelve-hour period are the numbers displayed in consecutive order (for example, 1:23)?

13

At the annual high-school baked goods sale, Mr. Ramsey sold sixty pies during the six-day sale. Each day, he sold four more pies than he did on the previous day. How many pies were sold on the first day?

14

A school was trying to raise money for a class trip by having students pay 1.00 to guess the number of jellybeansin a jar. Adam guessed there were forty-three, Bill guessed thirty-four, and Carl guessed forty-one. One person was off by six, another was off by three, and another was off by one. How many jellybeans were in the jar?

15

A banker had a scale that was only balanced when there were three gold bars on one side of the scale and one gold bar and a ten kilogram weight on the other side. Assuming all the gold bars weigh the same amount, how much does one gold bar weigh?

16

Steve and Lisa each have a bag containing the same number of marbles. How many marbles must Steve give Lisa so that Lisa will have ten more marbles than Steve?

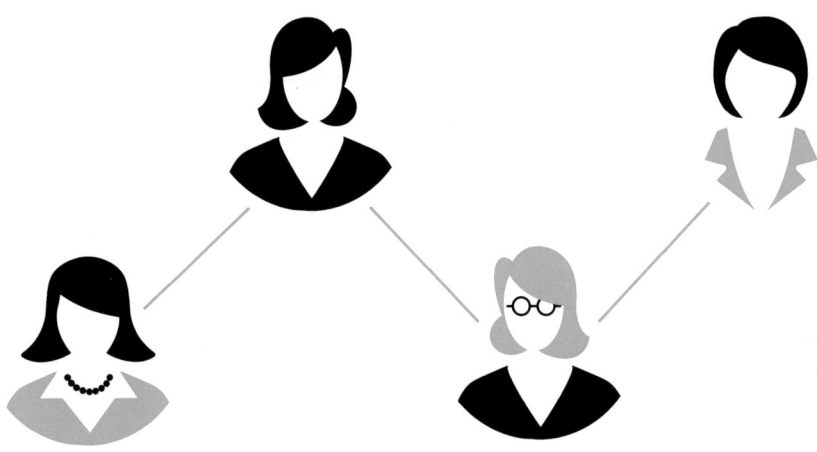

17

There were four women in the lobby waiting to interview for the same job. They shook hands with each other just once. How many handshakes were made?

18

Under the Christmas tree there were three presents—one for Samantha, one for Maria, and one for Louisa. Each present was wrapped with a different color paper, either red, green, or silver. There was also a different color bow on each present, either red, green, or gold. Using only the following two statements, determine the color of wrapping paper and bow that was on each of the presents.

1. Samantha's present had a green bow.

2. Louisa's present was the only one without contrasting colors of bow and paper.

19

The Moore family had twelve people over for caramel apples but they only made seven apples. How did they divide the seven caramel apples so that everyone had equal portions? Each apple cannot be cut into more than four pieces.

20

Mark and Bryan both have gardens of equal size in their front yard. Bryan decides to plant a single weed in Mark's garden so it won't look as nice. The weed doubles every day, and within thirty days Mark's garden is completely covered in weeds. If we assume the weed doubles in number every day, how many days will it take Bryan's garden to be completely covered in weeds when Mark plants two weeds in her garden?

21

If each of Peter's sons has twice as many sisters as brothers and each of his daughters has just as many sisters as brothers, how many sons and daughters does Peter have?

22

If the minute hand had just passed the hour hand, how long would it take until the next time this happens?

23

A cereal company is offering a magic decoder ring to anyone who sends in enough box tops. Jess and Courtney both want a ring, but Jess needs seven more box tops and Courtney needs one more. They thought of combining their box tops to get one ring, but they still don't have enough. How many box tops are needed for one ring?

24

Trish decided to go on a shopping spree. At the shoe store, she spent half of what she had plus 6.00 for a pair of boots. At the clothing store, she spent half of what was left plus 4.00 for a scarf. At the candy store, she spent half of what remained plus 2.00 for an ice cream cone. She had 7.00 left over. How much did she have originally?

25

There are nine jars, each containing a different type of liquid, but the labels have all fallen off. Knowing nothing about the contents, a passerby reapplies the labels at random. What is the expected number of correctly labeled jars?

26

A single-elimination billiards tournament is held for 100 players. How many matches will be played before a winner is crowned?

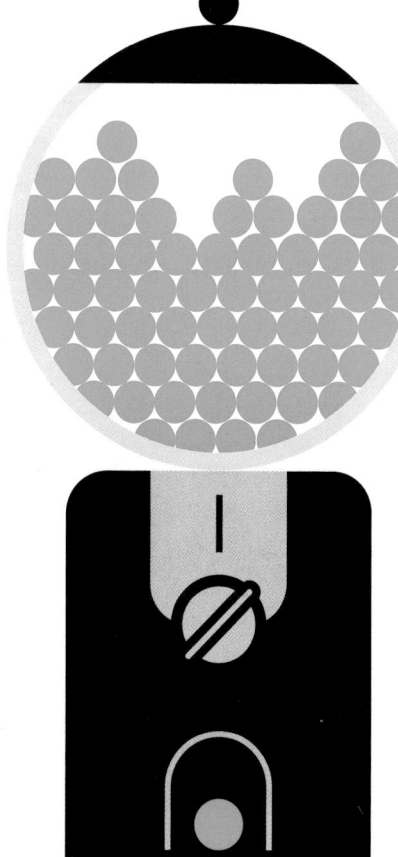

27

If 1,000 gumballs cost 20.00, how much would ten gumballs cost?

28

A weightless and perfectly flexible rope is hung over a weightless, frictionless pulley attached to the roof of a building. At one end is a weight that exactly counterbalances an orangutan at the other end. If the orangutan begins to climb, what will happen to the weight?

29

Olivia practices playing the piano one hour a day from Monday through Friday. How many hours must she practice on Saturday in order to have an average of two hours a day for the six-day period?

30

On a busy night in downtown, the valet parked 320 cars. Twenty-one tipped him 1.00, half of the remaining seventy-nine percent tipped him 2.00, and the rest did not tip at all. How much money did the valet make?

31

Amelia was looking in her closet, trying to figure out how many handbags she owned. All her bags are gold except two. All her bags are brown except two. All her bags are white except two. How many handbags does Trish have?

32

At the office party, George and Ava were planning on handing out jellybeans. They were hungry, however, and George had already eaten half of the jellybeans when Ava ate half the remaining jellybeans plus three more. There were no jellybeans left. How many jellybeans did they take to the office party?

33

A car dealer in Birmingham spent 20,000 for some used cars. He sold them for 27,500, making an average of 1,500 on each car. How many cars did he sell?

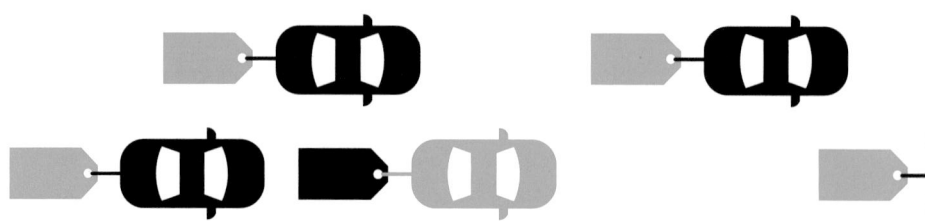

34

Dan and Craig were playing pool for 1.00 a game at a New Orleans pool hall. At the end of the day, Dan won 4.00 and Craig won three times. How many games did they play?

35

If Bill is taller than Mick and shorter than John, who is the tallest of the three?

36

Emily is now as old as Mia was eight years ago. Who is older?

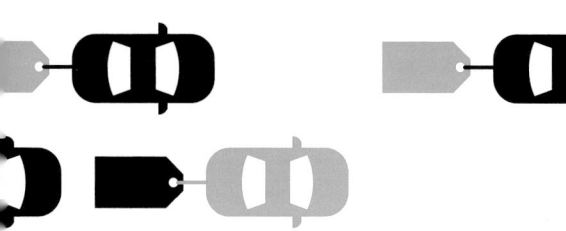

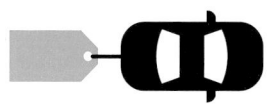

37

Mary Ellen was having a garage sale in Washington, DC and someone came by and bought the lawnmower. The person paid 100.00 for it and paid with a check. Before leaving, he decided he didn't want the lawnmower; he wanted the 75.00 chainsaw instead. Mary Ellen gave the person 25.00 change and he left. The check later bounced and she was charged a 25.00 overdraft fee by her bank. If the chainsaw originally cost her 50.00, how much did she lose?

38

During naptime, Juan was sleeping between Miguel and Enriqué. Ricardo was sleeping on Enriqué's right. Who was Enriqué sleeping between?

39

Jack sells desks and chairs in Calgary. The desks cost twenty-five times as much as the chairs do. Jack sold ten items, and one-fifth of them were desks. If the desks cost 100.00 for two, how much money did Jack earn?

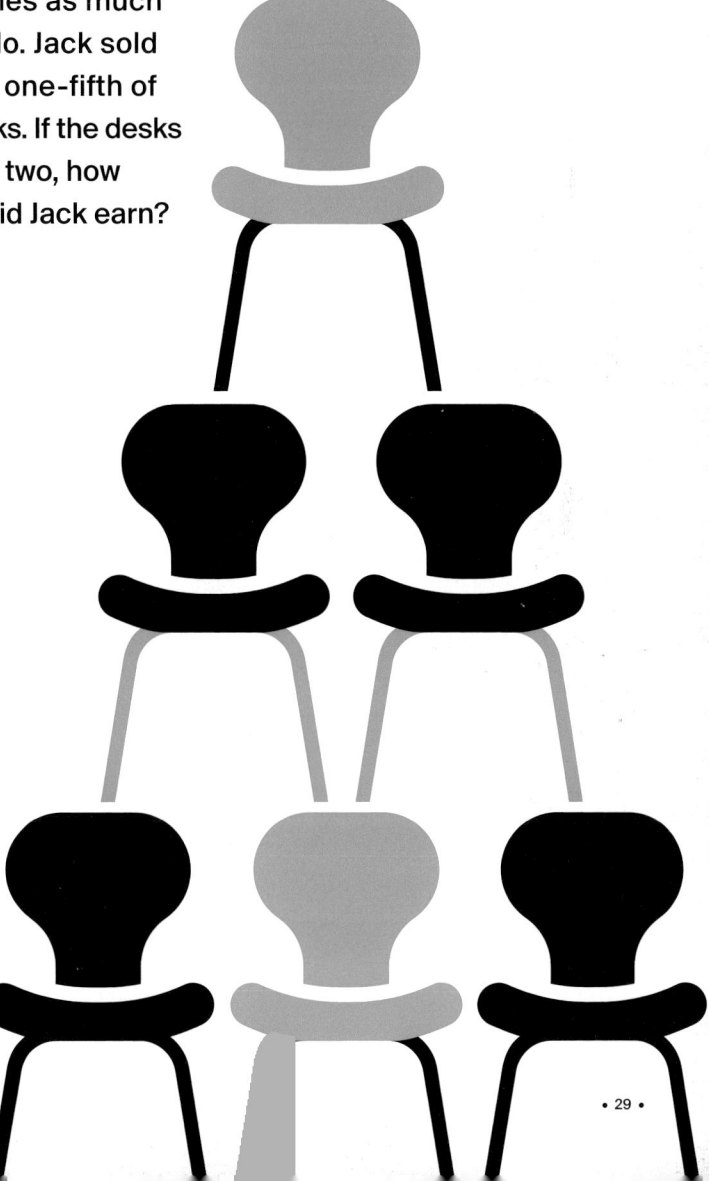

40

Tobias was an eccentric man who decided to give his fortune away to the winner of a horse race. In the rules, the winner was the one who came in last. Tobias didn't want the race to last forever, so he came up with an idea to prevent the jockeys from deliberately riding slowly to place last. What was Tobias's idea?

41

How many times does the minute hand pass the hour hand between noon/12:00 and midnight/24:00 on a normal clock?

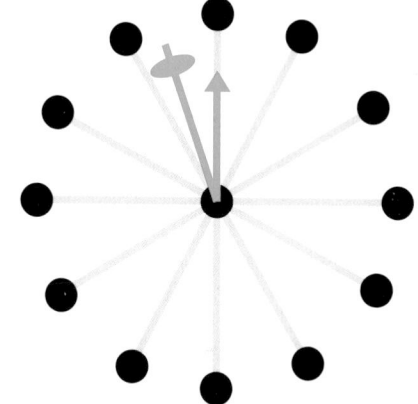

42

Is it possible for Ella to have seven children if half of them are girls?

43

At the local shopping mall, Muhammad went into five stores, eventually spending all his money. In each store, he spent 1.00 more than half of what he had when he came in. How much money did Muhammad have when he went into the first store?

44

Every hour on the hour a train leaves Minneapolis for Chicago and a train leaves Chicago for Minneapolis.

The trains all travel at the same speed and the trip from Minneapolis to Chicago takes five hours. How many trains pass by each other on one trip?

45

While running a 3,000-meter race on an indoor track, Oscar notices that one-fifth of the runners in front of him plus five-sixths of the runners in back of him add up to the total number of runners. How many people are running in the race?

46

The director of an orphanage wanted to get a present for all the kids who didn't already have every toy. The orphanage has 100 kids: eighty-five have a bicycle, seventy-five have a football, seventy have a baseball cap, and eighty have toy spinners. What is the least possible number of kids who own a bicycle, football, baseball cap, and toy spinners?

47

For an international summit, fifteen representatives from the United States, France, Britain, and Germany met in Switzerland. Each country sent a different number of representatives and each country is represented by at least one person. Britain and France sent a total of six representatives. France and Germany sent a total of seven representatives. Which country sent four representatives?

48

Bill and Lilly are preparing to take a 4,000-kilometer trip in their car throughout the United Kingdom. The car has four tires and each tire lasts only 1,500 kilometers. How many tires will Bill and Lilly go through if we assume the tires on the car are brand new?

N

49

Jessica is planning on running the Boston marathon and the New York City marathon. Jessica finds a store that has sneakers on sale and she wants to buy enough sneakers to get through both marathons. If each marathon is twenty-six miles and each pair of sneakers lasts ten miles, how many pairs of sneakers should Jessica buy?

50

Three people are having a dinner party in Montreal. Blake shows up with five dishes and his friend Jackson brings three dishes. Abigail stops by with no dishes but decides to sit down and eat with them. Abigail pays 20.00 as her share. If we assume that all the dishes have the same value, how can the 20.00 be split between Blake and Jackson?

51

In the barnyard there are goats and chickens. In all, there are 22 heads and 72 feet. How many chickens and goats are there in the barnyard?

52

Christopher is on a ladder painting a wall. He starts on the middle rung, goes up six rungs, goes down eight rungs, up three rungs, and up twelve more rungs to reach the top bar of the ladder. How many rungs are there on the ladder?

53

Angela is interviewing for new jobs in Sydney and has narrowed it down to two possible companies. The first company offers 27,000 per year with a 1,000 per year raise given twice a year. The second company is also offering 27,000 with a 2,000 per year raise given once a year. Which job should Angela choose?

54

A sushi restaurant in London buys twenty fish for 10.00 each. The owner knows that fifty percent of the fish will go bad before being served. Each fish creates ten servings. What price must they charge per serving in order to make a one hundred percent profit on their initial investment?

55

Erik decides to climb Mt. Everest with the help of the local Sherpas. It will take him six days to reach the summit, but he can only carry four days' worth of food in his pack. If the Sherpas can also only carry four days' worth of food, how many Sherpas will Erik need to reach the summit?

56

You are in a strange country that uses a currency system you've never seen before. In your pocket you have only seven-cent coins and eleven-cent coins. What is the most expensive item that cannot be purchased with any combination of the two coins?

57

Noah goes to his bank in Miami to cash his 1,500.00 paycheck, but the bank is out of certain bills. The teller cashes Noah's check using a certain number of 1.00 bills and ten times as many 5.00 bills, and a certain number of 10.00 bills and twice as many 50.00 bills. How many bills of each kind does the teller pay out?

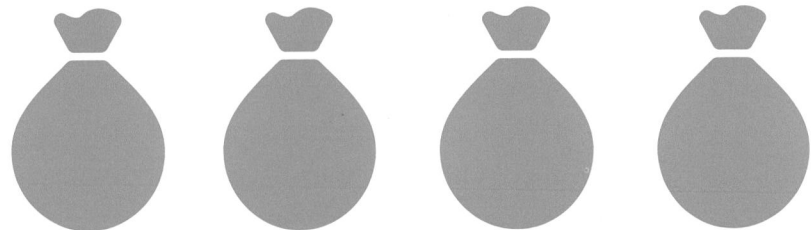

58

Elena decided to run twenty miles to warm up for the marathon. She ran the first half at five-miles-per hour and ran the second half at ten-miles-per hour. What was her average speed?

59

You are given five identical sacks containing ten gold coins each. All the gold coins weigh one pound each, except for the coins in the fifth sack. In the fifth sack, all the gold coins weigh nine-tenths of a pound.

How can you figure out which sack has the lighter coins in it using a single-tray scale if you are only allowed to use the scale once?

60

During baseball spring training, Derek and Bernie were practicing hitting baseballs. His first time at bat, Derek hit seventy-five out of a hundred pitches. Then Bernie hit seventy-five out of a hundred pitches. On Derek's second turn at bat, he hit thirty-five of the fifty pitches thrown. Bernie didn't take a second turn at bat. Who had the best average for the day—Derek or Bernie?

61

Ella is playing with blocks in her room. She decides to stack up all the blocks so that each row has one less block than the row below. Ella has fifty-five blocks total and she wants to end up with just one block on top. How many should she put on the bottom row?

62

One cup of green tea has twenty-five percent more caffeine than one cup of coffee. If Jacob drinks five cups of coffee and Benjamin drinks four cups of green tea, who drank more caffeine?

63

All of Alison's pets are cats except one. All of her pets are goldfish except one. How many cats and goldfish does Alison have?

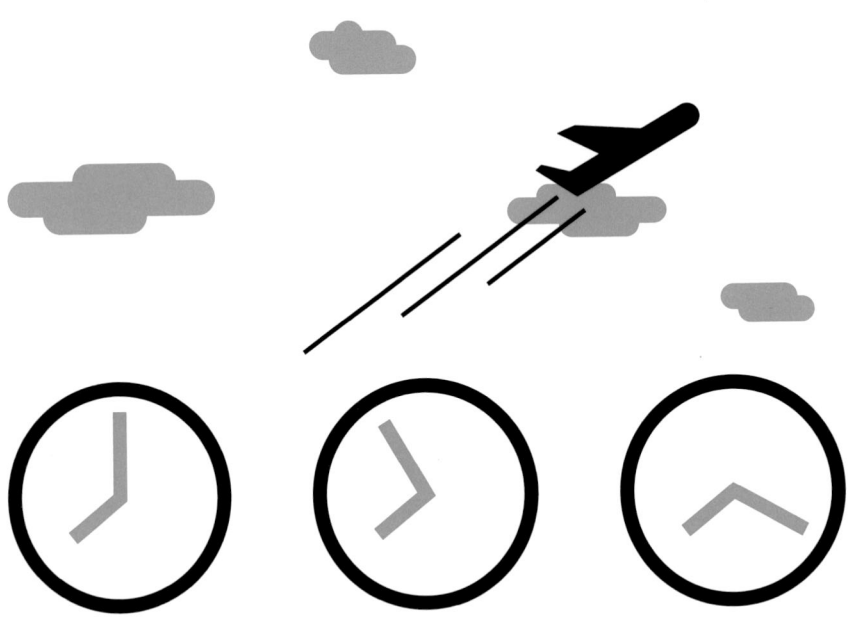

64

At Toronto Pearson International Airport there are three clocks in the terminal. Clock A says it's 8:00, clock B says it's 8:50, and clock C says it's 8:20. One of the clocks is twenty minutes fast, one is slow, and one is off by half an hour. What is the actual time?

65

It takes seventeen minutes for seventeen bakers to bake seventeen cookies. How many bakers do you need to bake fifty-one cookies in fifty-one minutes?

66

Charlotte has two boxes. Each box holds four spoons and four forks. Without looking, you draw one piece of silverware from each box. What are the chances that at least one of the pieces of silverware you draw is a spoon?

67

In a group of 100 students, seventy lost a notebook, seventy five lost a pencil, eighty five lost a calculator, and eighty lost a ruler. What is the minimum number of students who must have lost all four?

68

Coco, the cat, is heavier than Lulu, another cat. Winston weighs more than Fluffy but less than Rocky. Fluffy weighs more than Lulu. Rocky weighs less than Coco.

List the cats in the order of their weights, starting with the heaviest.

69

A new brand of oatmeal cookies has ninety percent less fat than the regular brand. How many of the reduced fat cookies would I have to eat to ingest the same amount of fat that would be in one regular oatmeal cookie?

70

Amelia was walking down the street in San Diego and found 4.00 on the sidewalk. She put the 4.00 in her purse with the money she had before she found it and she now had five times the amount of money she would have had if she had lost 4.00. How much money did Amelia have before she found the 4.00

71

A snail is at the bottom of a ten-foot well. She climbs three feet a day, but during the night, while resting, she slips back two feet. At this rate, how many days will it take the snail to climb out of the well?

72

Jean-Pierre began teaching his first French cooking class and he has fewer than 500 students. One-third of the students is a whole number. So are one-fourth, one-fifth, and one-seventh of the students. How many students are enrolled in Jean-Pierre's cooking class?

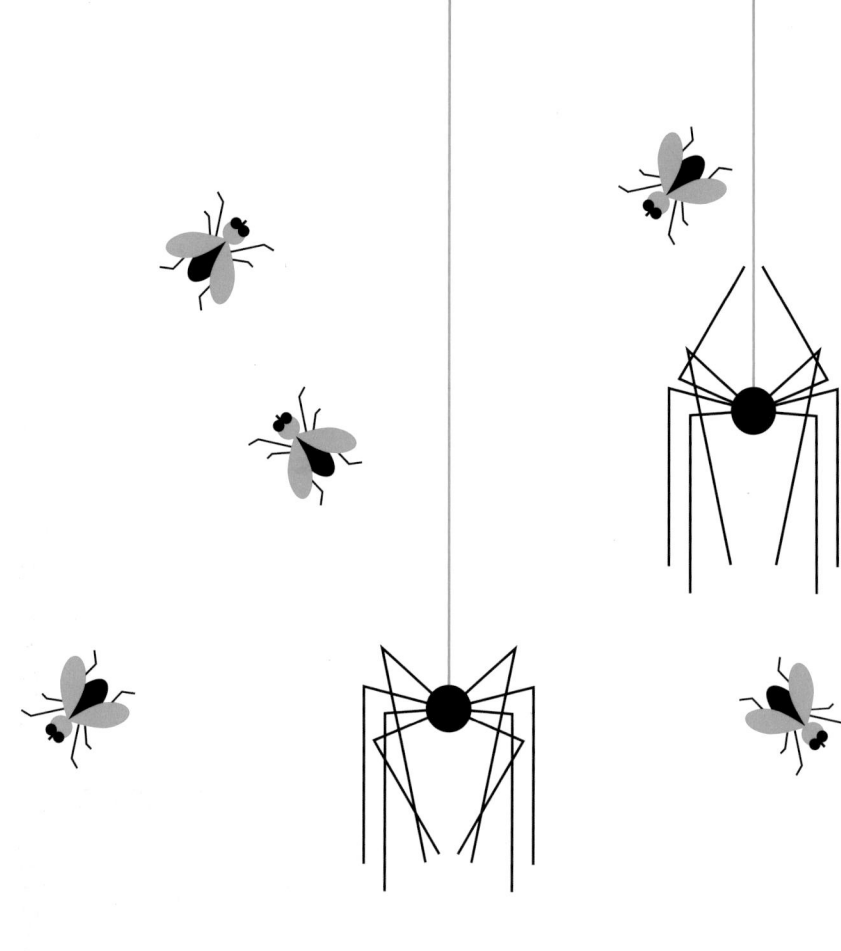

73

Beth is twice as old as her brother and half as old as her father. In twenty-two years, her brother will be half as old as his father. How old is Beth now?

74

If you have a group of six-legged flies and eight-legged spiders and there are forty-eight legs in total, how many flies and how many spiders are there in the group?

75

Andy, Bill, Chris, Drake, and Eric are mice learning to go through a maze. Each time a mouse reaches the end of the maze, it gets a pellet of food.

So far, Andy has gotten four more pellets than Bill. Bill has gotten seven fewer pellets than Chris. Chris has gotten five more pellets than Drake, and Drake has gotten three more pellets than Eric. Bill and Drake have gotten ten pellets between them. How many times has each mouse gone through the maze so far?

76

Jack has six brothers. Each brother is four years older than his next younger brother. The oldest brother is three times as old as his youngest brother. How old are each of the brothers?

77

Two people can make two hats in two hours. How many people are needed to make twelve hats in six hours?

79

Anthony, Bill, Carl, and Dave all decided to start taking singing lessons. Carl took twice as many lessons as Bill. Anthony took four lessons more than Dave but three fewer than Carl. Dave took fifteen lessons altogether. How many singing lessons did Bill take?

78

Scarlett went to the candy store and was able to buy exactly 100 pieces of candy for a dollar. Some of her candy cost ten cents a piece; some of her candy cost three cents a piece; and some of her candy cost one cent for two pieces. How many pieces of each kind of candy did Scarlett buy?

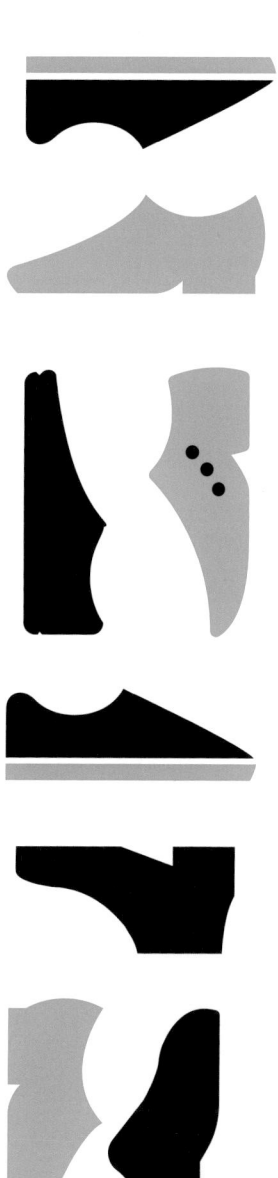

80

Patrick loves his shoes. He has ten pairs of shoes in five different colors. Patrick is a particularly lazy person, however, and just tosses his shoes in a bin when he takes them off. He needs to go away for a weekend on business, but he put off packing until really early in the morning. It's still dark outside and he can't see the color of the shoes in the bins. How many individual shoes will he have to take out of the bin to be sure that he has at least two of the same color?

81

John went to Melbourne and bought a painting for 2,500. When he came home, his friend Lucas saw the painting and gave John 3,500 for it. A few days later, John bought the painting back for 4,500, thinking it would be worth more someday. He took it to a local art dealer, who offered him 5,500 for it, so John sold it to the art dealer. Did John make money or lose money in the end?

82

Dan's weekly salary in Toronto is 70.00 less than Liam's, whose weekly salary is 50.00 more than Sophia's. If Sophia earns 280.00 per week, how much does Dan earn per week?

83

Juanita loved to put jigsaw puzzles together. She managed to try at least one puzzle per day. For every puzzle she completed, she gave herself two points, and for every puzzle she couldn't complete, she subtracted three points. After thirty days of putting together puzzles, Juanita had a score of zero. How many puzzles was she able to complete?

84

Patti moved to Seattle and wasn't used to all the rain. She decided to make a rain gauge to measure the amount of rain for one week. It rained each day that week, starting on Monday, and each day the amount of rain in the gauge doubled. By the following Sunday, the rain gauge was completely filled. On which day was the rain gauge half-filled?

85

A car dealership reduced the price of one of its models by twenty five percent for its Year End Sale. By what percentage of the sales price must it be increased to put the car back to its original price?

86

Brian decided to propose to Andrea and went shopping for a ring. At the first jewelry store, he found a one-carat ring for 3,000. At the second jewelry store, he found the same one-carat ring for 3,500. The first jewelry store had a twenty percent fee for any rings that were returned and the second jewelry store had no fees for returns. If there is a fifty percent chance that Andrea will say no, which jewelry store should Brian buy the ring at to maximize his risk/reward?

87

During a summit meeting, John is in charge of protecting two diplomats, one from France and one from Spain. John has a twenty-five percent chance of thwarting an assassination attempt against the French diplomat and a fifty percent chance of thwarting an assassination attempt against the Spanish diplomat. If there are six people at the summit who are going to attempt to assassinate the French diplomat and ten people attempting to assassinate the Spanish diplomat, which diplomat is in greater danger of being assassinated?

88

Michael had a job in the produce section of a grocery store stacking oranges. His boss told him to stack thirty-five oranges so that each row of oranges would have one more than the row above it. How many rows of oranges did Michael have when he was finished?

89

There is a flagpole in the middle of Lake Tahoe. Half of the flagpole is in the lake bed, another one-third of it is covered by water, and ten feet of the flagpole is sticking out of the water. What is the total length of the flagpole?

90

At Springfield High School, everyone plays on a sports team. There are five more soccer players than baseball players. There are three more students on the track team than on the baseball team. There are two more football players than hockey players. There are three more students on the track team than on the football team. The number of baseball and football players equals eight. How many players are on each team?

91

It takes Mario one hour to install carpet on a bedroom floor that is nine-feet wide and twelve-feet long. How long will it take him to put carpet on the living room floor, which is twice as wide and twice as long?

92

Hill Valley High School has an annual tug-of-war game among the sports players. With three football players on one side and two baseball players on the other side, the game ended in a tie. Similarly, with three soccer players on one side and four baseball players on the other side, the game ended in a tie. Which side, if either, will win if one side has five football players and the other side has two soccer players?

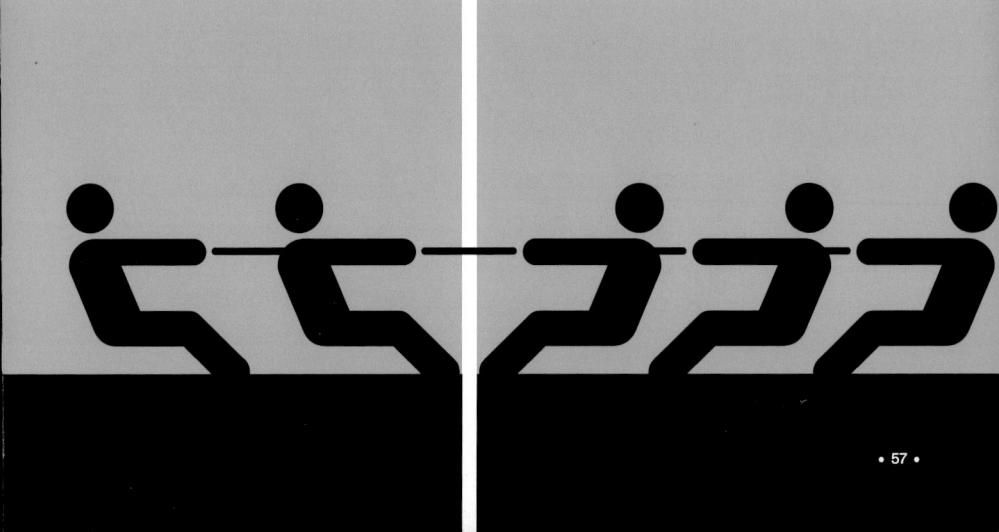

93

Vince drove to from Chicago to Madison at the rate of twenty miles an hour. When he got to Madison, he realized he forgot his wallet and rushed home at forty miles an hour. The whole trip took him six hours. How many miles is it from Chicago to Madison?

94

Tommy and Ralph both own clothing stores selling the same items. Tommy sells the same pair of shoes as Ralph, and they both sell for 100.00. Tommy decides to lower the price by twenty-five percent and Ralph counters by lowering the price thirty percent. When Tommy finds out that Ralph lowered the price on his shoes, Tommy lowers the price of his by another fifteen percent. Ralph in turn lowers the price of his by ten percent. Who is selling the shoes for less?

95

Charlotte is playing roulette in Las Vegas. If there are thirty-six numbers on the wheel, figure out which two-digit number Charlotte has placed her bet on, given the following facts:

The number is divisible by three.

The sum of the digits in this number lies between four and eight.

It is an odd number.

When the digits in this number are multiplied together, the total lies between four and eight.

96

At the local wholesale shopping market they sell large containers of orange juice and apple juice.

On the shelves there are six containers, each holding the following amounts:

Container A: thirty quarts

Container B: thirty-two quarts

Container C: thirty-six quarts

Container D: thirty-eight quarts

Container E: forty quarts

Container F: sixty-two quarts

Five of the containers hold orange juice, and one container holds apple juice.

Two customers come into the market and the first customer buys two containers of orange juice. The second customer buys twice as much orange juice as the first customer. Which container is holding the apple juice?

97

You have a spool with 100 meters of wire. You need 100 lengths of wire that are one-meter long each. If it takes you one second to measure and cut each meter, how long will it take you to come up with 100 pieces of wire?

98

Trent, Mary, and Shawn all work in a factory. Trent earns half of what Mary makes. Shawn earns three times what Trent makes. If the three of them together earn 144.00 a day, how much are each of them making in a day?

99

If ten hens can produce fifteen eggs in a week, how many eggs can fifteen hens produce in two weeks?

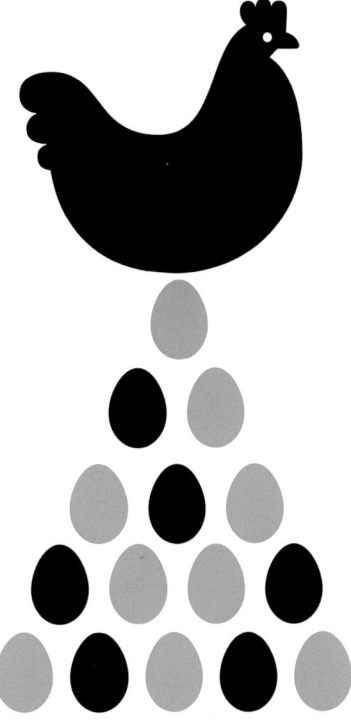

100

Using a garden hose, how can you measure out one liter of water if you only have a three-liter and a five-liter jug?

101

Chris is thirty-three years old today. This is three times as old as Paul was when Chris was the age that Paul is today. How old is Paul?

101

A certain book costs 12.00 more in hardcover than in paperback. If the paperback price is two-thirds of the hardcover price, how much does the book cost in hardcover?

zzz...

103

Georgia takes the subway to work each day. She gets on the subway at the first stop and usually takes a nap. Georgia falls asleep when the subway still has twice as far to go as it has already gone. Midway through the ride, Georgia wakes up to check her watch. When she starts to doze off again, the subway still has half the distance to go that it has already traveled. Georgia wakes up at the end of the ride and goes to work. What portion of the ride did Georgia sleep through?

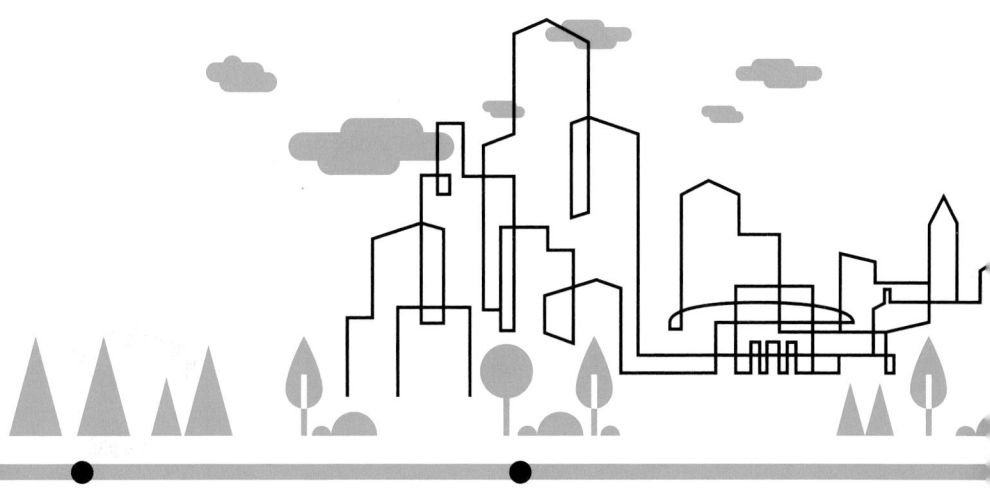

104

Justine is planning to drive across the country. She is going to drive a few miles on the first day and add twenty more miles on each subsequent day. The total trip is going to take her 1,080 miles. How many miles will she drive on the last day?

105

Five retirees meet every week for a game of bridge. They use a table with six chairs. If they choose a different seating arrangement each week and exhaust every possibility, how long have the retirees played bridge together?

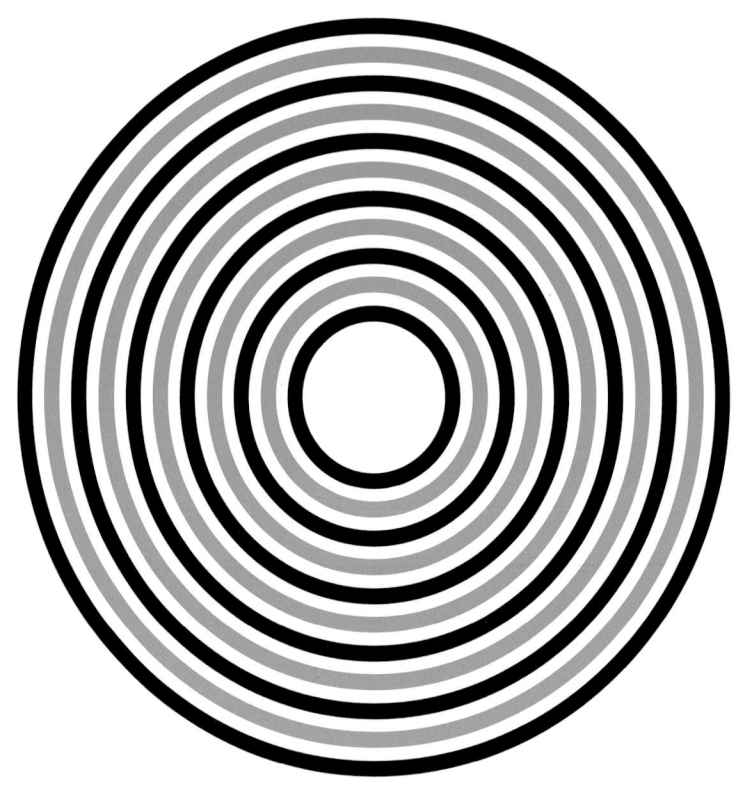

106

Tim and Greg are roofers. Tim makes 100.00 a day and Greg makes 75.00 a day. If they just finished a roofing job in which they billed the customer 1,000 for labor, how many days did they work on the roof?

107

A jeweler is producing gold rings. For every eleven rings she makes, she has enough scrap gold to be melted into one extra ring. How many rings can she make from the scrap after making 250 gold rings?

108

A giant gumball machine has seventy-one gumballs left. The flavors are lemon, raspberry, orange, and grape. There are twice as many lemon gumballs as raspberry ones. There is one less orange-flavored gumball than raspberry-flavored, and there are six fewer grape gumballs than lemon ones. How many gumballs do you have to take from the machine to have at least two of one flavor?

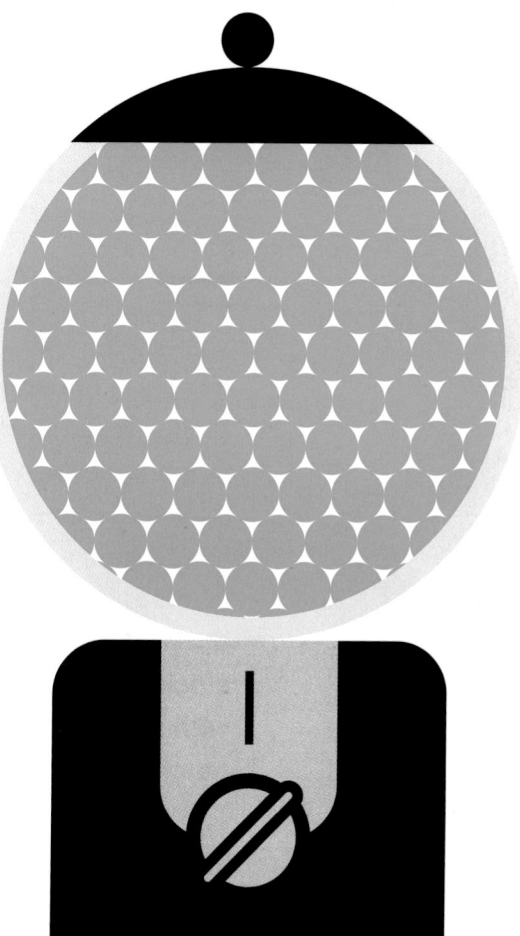

109

At the Tokyo Fish Market, one sturgeon weighs 120 pounds, and one swordfish weighs thirty-six pounds. What is the weight of one halibut and one grouper, when the grouper and the swordfish together weigh as much as the sturgeon and the halibut?

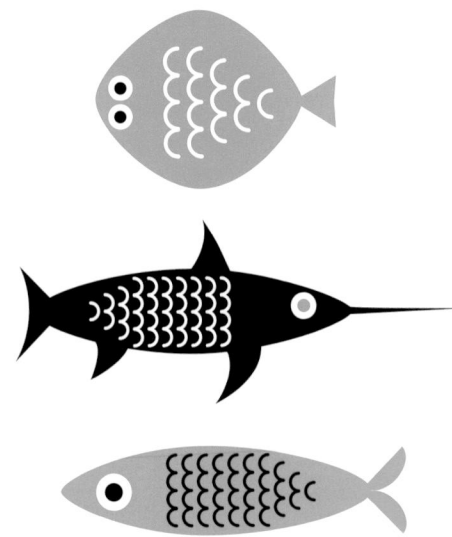

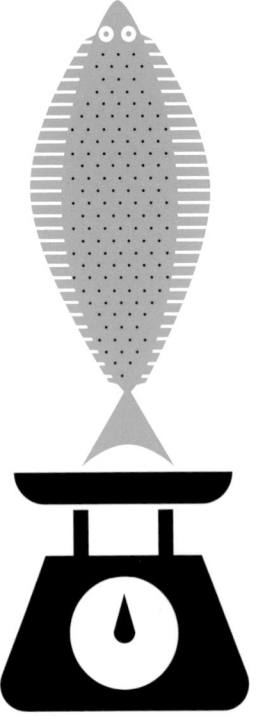

110

It is noon at Paddington Station when Charlie asks the ticket seller when the next train to Oxford leaves. He is told the next train leaves when the minute hand and the hour hand of the station clock will be exactly lined up with each other again. How much time does Charlie have before the next train leaves?

111

Mary has seven people at her birthday party and everyone wants a piece of cake. How can Mary cut the cake into eight pieces if she's only allowed to make three straight cuts and she can't move the pieces as she cuts them?

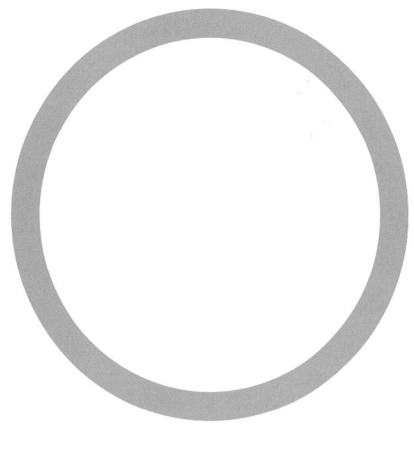

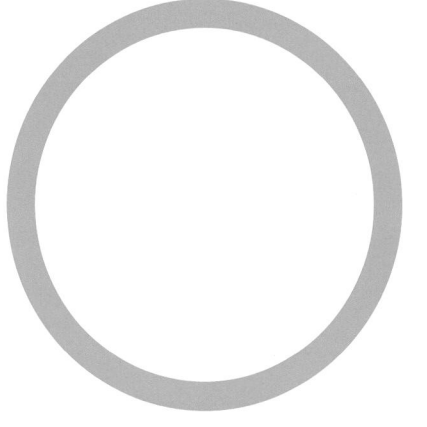

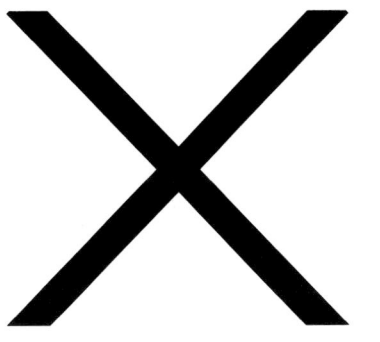

112

Is it possible to put six X's on a Tic Tac Toe board without making three-in-a-row in any direction?

113

At a local farmfield, it takes ten cows twenty days to eat all the grass. If fifteen cows are in the field, the grass will be gone in ten days. When will the grass be gone if there are twenty-five cows in the field?

114

Using a budget of 100.00, Jim needs to buy 100 staplers for his company. He has to buy exactly 100 staplers and he must use the entire 100.00. If the jumbo staplers cost 6.00, the regular staplers cost 3.00, and the tiny staplers cost 0.10, how many of each does Jim have to buy?

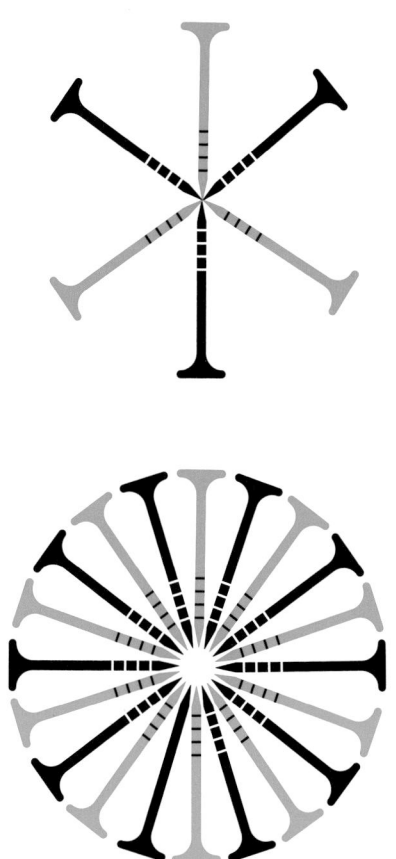

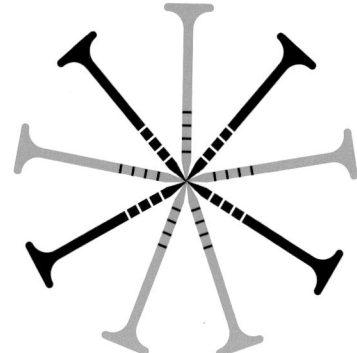

115

Olivia went back-to-school shopping and spent half her money on a new jacket. She then spent half of that amount on a pair of sneakers. If she has 25.00 left, how much did she spend?

116

At the hardware store, you can buy nails in boxes of six, nine, and twenty. What is the largest number of nails that it is not possible to obtain by purchasing some combination of boxes?

117

A box contains two coins. One coin is heads on both sides and the other is heads on one side and tails on the other. One coin is selected from the box at random and the face of one side is observed. If the face is heads, what is the probability that the other side is heads?

118

Using just a four-minute hourglass and a seven-minute hourglass, how can you measure nine minutes?

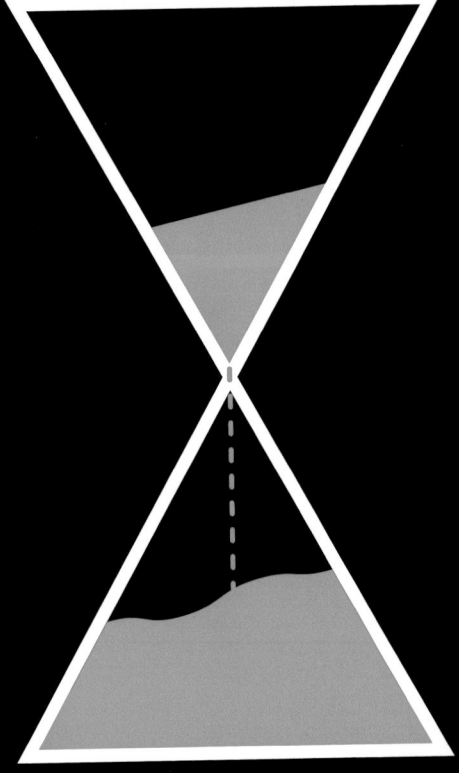

119

Bill and Mick are both collectors of vintage watches. If Bill were to sell Mick seven watches, then Bill would have exactly as many watches as Mick. On the other hand, if Mick were to sell Bill seven watches, then Bill would have exactly twice as many watches as Mick. How many watches does each person have?

120

Richard can eat 100 peanuts in half a minute, and Marion can eat half as many in twice the length of time. How many peanuts can Richard and Marion eat in fifteen seconds?

121

Maxime and Dan were telling their friend the results of a horse race. There were three horses in the race, Quick Ted, Atomic Angie, and Dragonlady. Maxime told his friend that Quick Ted had won the race and Atomic Angie came in second. Dan told his friend that Dragonlady had won the race and Quick Ted had come in second.

In reality, however, neither Maxime or Dan had told their friend the actual results of the race. Each of them had given one correct statement and one false statement. In what order did the three horses actually finish?

122

Distillery owner Mr. McFadden recently passed away. In his will, he left twenty-one barrels of scotch (seven of which are full, seven of which are half-full, and seven of which are empty) to his three sons. However, the scotch and barrels must be split so that each son has the same number of full barrels, the same number of half-full barrels, and the same number of empty barrels. If there are no measuring devices handy, how can the barrels and scotch be evenly divided?

123

Karen went to the farmers' market to buy fruit. She ended up buying three boxes of fruit: one full of cherries, one full of strawberries, and one containing a mixture of both. The farmer who sold her the fruit put labels on the boxes, but she was in a hurry and put the incorrect label on each box.

How can you label the boxes correctly if you are only allowed to take and look at just one piece of fruit from just one of the boxes?

124

You are in a room with two doors. Behind one door is a lion that will eat you if you open it. The second door will get you out of the room. In the room with you are two men who know which door is the safe one. One of the two men always tells the truth and one of the men always tells lies. If you can ask only one of the men one question, what question could you ask that would give you the information you need to choose the correct door?

125

Zack showed up at the local race track just after the first race ended. He asked his buddy Brad what the results of the race were, and Brad said:

"Silver Wagon finished before Master David and after Say It Fast.

Say It Fast tied with Silver Wagon if, and only if, Sir Oscar did not tie with Lion Heart.

Silver Wagon finished as many places after Lion Heart as Lion Heart finished after Say It Fast if, and only if, Say It Fast finished before Master David."

How did the five horses finish the race?

126

Yvette, Erin, and Dan joined a local bird-watching club and went to the park to look for birds. Each of them saw one bird that neither of the others did. Each pair saw one bird that the third did not. One bird was seen by all three. Of the birds Yvette saw, two were yellow. Of the birds Erin saw, three were yellow. Of the birds Dan saw, four were yellow. How many yellow birds were seen in all?

127

Darren, Tom, Rob, and Matt went to a black-tie benefit. When they arrived, they checked their coats, hats, gloves, and canes at the door (each of the gentlemen had one of each). When they checked out, there was a mix up, and each of the men ended up with exactly one article of clothing belonging to each one of the four. Darren and Tom ended up with their own coats, Rob ended up with his own hat, and Matt ended up with his own gloves. Darren did not end up with Rob's cane. Whose coat, hat, gloves, and cane did each of the gentlemen end up with?

128

Troy is an explosives expert who is wiring a cave to explode. He has forty-five minutes to get out of the cave before it blows up, but he doesn't have a watch. All he has are two fuses, each of which will burn up in exactly one hour. They are not of the same length and width as each other, so he can't measure a half hour by noting when one fuse is half burned. Using these two fuses, how can Troy measure forty-five minutes?

129

A spider eats three flies a day. Until the spider fills his quota, a fly has a fifty-percent chance of survival if he attempts to pass the web. Assuming five flies have already made the attempt to pass, what is the probability that the sixth fly will survive the attempt?

130

An office has twenty-seven employees. If there are seven more women than men in the office, how many employees are women?

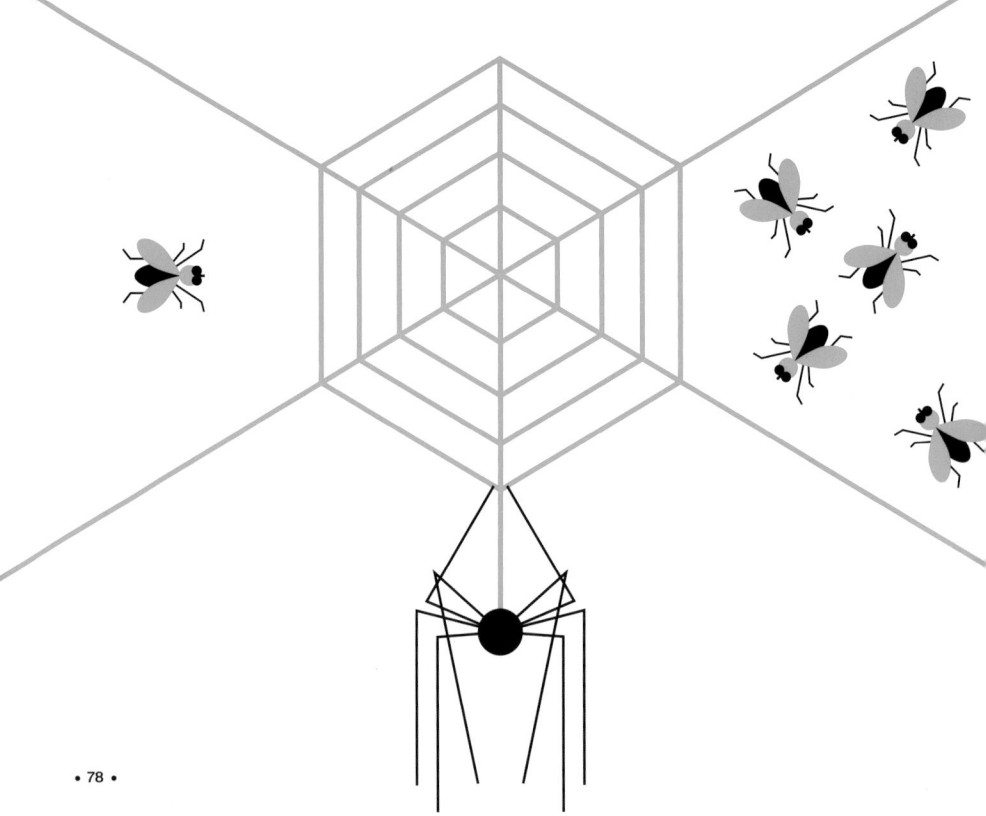

131

Ingrid goes to a department store to buy a screen protector, protective case, and headphones for her computer. After some shopping around, she finds the best deals for each. The sum of the price of the headphones and six times the cost of the screen protector minus three times the cost of the protective case is seventeen dollars. Also, four times the cost of the protective case minus twice the cost of the headphones plus seven times the cost of the screen protector is thirteen dollars. In addition, seventeen times the cost of the protective case plus thirty times the cost the screen protector minus eight times the cost of the headphones equals sixty-three dollars. How much did Ingrid spend at the mall?

132

Erik has 100.00 more than Ron. After Eric spends 20.00 on groceries, Erik has five times as much money as Ron. How much money does Ron have?

133

Nico purchased a camera, a ruler, and an ice cream bar for 53.00. He paid 52.00 more for the camera than the ice cream bar, and the ruler cost twice as much as the ice cream bar. What did he pay for each?

134

There are enough gumballs in a bag to give twelve gumballs to each of the twenty children, with no gumballs left over. If five children do not want any gumballs, how many gumballs can be given to each of the others?

135

A NYC subway car passes an average of three stations every ten minutes. At this rate, how many stations will it pass in one hour?

136

Imagine that you have three boxes, one containing two black marbles, one containing two white marbles, and the third, one black marble and one white marble. The boxes were labeled for their contents—BB, WW, and BW—but someone has switched the labels so that every box is now incorrectly labeled. You are allowed to take one marble at a time out of any box, without looking inside, and by this process of sampling you are to determine the contents of all three boxes. What is the smallest number of drawings needed to do this?

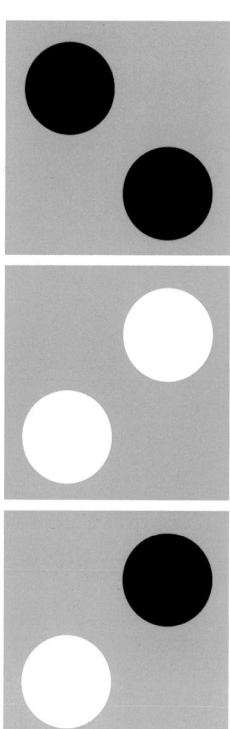

137

A rancher is given 100.00 to buy 100 animals. She must spend all 100.00 and have no change left over. Cows cost 10.00, pigs cost 5.00, and chickens cost 0.50 apiece. How many of each animal does she have to buy to spend all 100.00 and have exactly 100 animals?

138

The stock of IBM has been selling for the last year in the range of 70.00–80.00. A year ago the price of IBM was less than or equal to the price of its competitor, Microsoft. Microsoft is now selling at exactly one-eighth of a point below its price last year, but IBM has declined so far it is only two-thirds the price of Microsoft now. What are the two currently selling at?

139

At Franklin High School, ten percent of the students use an illegal drug. A drug test yields the correct result ninety percent of the time, whether or not the student uses drugs. A random student is asked to take the drug test and the result is positive. What is the probability that he uses drugs?

140

A casino uses only 5.00 and 8.00 chips on its standard roulette wheel. What is the largest wager that cannot be placed?

141

During his five turns with the cue, a billiards player sank 100 balls. During each turn, he sank six more balls than he did during his previous turn. Can you figure out how many balls he sank during each of his five turns?

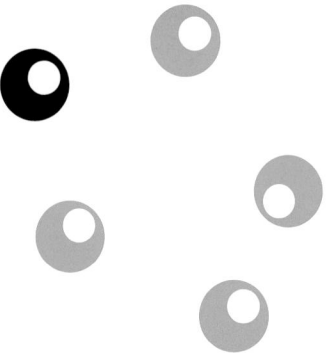

142

A company flew its employees to Las Vegas for the weekend. Some of the employees decided to go to a nightclub. The cover charge at the nightclub was 10.00 for men and 6.50 for women. Although there were more men than women at the club, the percentage of men who did not go was twice the percentage of women who did not go. Knowing this percentage and the total number of employees, one can deduce the total cover charge paid by the group. If there were between 60 and 100 employees in Las Vegas, how many went to the club?

143

A man is standing on a hill overlooking a calm lake. His eyes are 100 meters above the surface of the lake. He sees a balloon in the sky. He finds that the angle of elevation of the balloon is thirty degrees, and the angle of depression of the balloon's reflection in the lake is sixty degrees. What is the height of the balloon above the lake?

144

A half-kilometer-long train enters a tunnel that is ten kilometers long. If the train is traveling at thirty-five kilometers per hour, how long will it take for the entire train to pass through the tunnel?

145

Chris, Leila, Nico, and José are members of the Metropolitan Club. Every pair of members is together on one, and only one, committee in the club. Each committee has three members. What is the smallest possible total membership, and how many committees are there?

146

A store raised the price of their plasma TVs by twenty-five percent for the holidays. After the shopping season was over, they lowered the price by twenty-five percent. Is the price of the TV lower than before, the same, or higher?

147

Jason starts his own online business selling pool tables and he wants to hire Federal Express to ship the pool tables. FedEx has two trucks that can handle a pool table, one large and one small. Their large truck is twice as high, twice as wide, and twice as long as their small one. FedEx has decided to charge 500.00 per shipment for each delivery they make with a fully loaded small truck.

Assuming that charges are based on each truck's volume, what should FedEx charge for each delivery they make with a fully-loaded large truck?

148

A teacher brings in a bag of lollipops for her students. John takes three-fifths of the lollipops and Ken has three-fourths of Anne's share of the remaining lollipops. What fraction of the total number of lollipops does Anne have?

149

A poll was taken at a local town hall meeting to see what newspapers the citizens were reading. Sixty-four percent were reading the *Sun-Times*, twenty-two percent were reading the *Post*, and seven percent were reading both. What percentage of the citizens polled were reading no newspaper?

150

Isla was selling air conditioners during a five-day heat wave. She sold thirty air conditioners total, and each day she sold three more air conditioners than the day before. How many air conditioners did she sell the first day?

151

There are 100 contestants at a spelling bee and each contestant is either has blonde hair or brown hair. Given any two of the contestants, at least one is a blonde. How many of the contestants have blonde hair and how many have brown?

152

Ava is trying to figure out the weight of a wheel of cheese. She knows that one-fifth of a pound of cheese is perfectly balanced by two-fifths of a wheel of the same cheese. How much does the entire wheel of cheese weigh?

153

A farmer is trying to fill a small pond on her land so the livestock can drink. She hires two companies to fill the pond. One company can fill the pond in two hours, and another company can fill it in five hours. However, the ground soaks up the entire pond in six hours. With both companies filling the pond and the ground soaking up the water, how long will it take to fill the pond?

154

At a company's holiday party, one-third of the employees left early. Later on in the evening, two-fifths of the remaining employees left, and a few hours later, two-thirds of the remaining employees went home. If there are six employees still at the party, how many attended?

155

A box of chocolates can be divided equally among three, five, or thirteen people. What is the smallest number of chocolates the box can contain?

156

A delivery man named Jeff gets paid 500.00 for every delivery he makes on time. The only problem is, he has to speed to make the delivery on time. He gets pulled over for speeding twenty-five percent of the time. This makes him late for the delivery, which means he doesn't get paid, and he has to pay a 200.00 speeding ticket. How much is Jeff making on average per delivery?

157

Fernando is studying a type of bacteria that multiplies every minute. He places one bacteria strain in a Petri dish, and after one minute the bacteria splits. One minute later, the two bacteria split again. One minute after that, the four bacteria split, and so on. After three hours, the dish is halfway full. How much longer will it take to fill the dish completely?

158

Four friends decide to go out to the movies. When they arrive, there are four empty seats in the theater. How many different ways can the four friends combine to fill the seats?

159

If everyone on the South Side of Chicago owns an even number of cars, no one owns more than 100 cars, and no two people own the same number of cars, what is the maximum number of cars on the South Side?

160

Freckles the clown has just learned how to juggle four balls. How many throws must he make before the balls are returned to their original positions?

Freckles starts out with two balls in each hand and throws one ball from one hand, then another ball from the second hand, then the remaining ball from the first hand, and so on. Except for the first throw for each hand, there is a moment where the throwing hand no longer holds anything after each throw.

161

With the price of cigarettes skyrocketing, Danielle figured out that if she collected cigarette butts, she could make a cigarette from every five butts found. She found twenty-five butts, so how many cigarettes could she smoke?

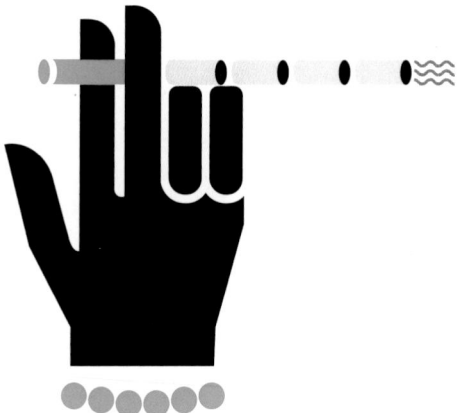

162

At the University of Virginia, there are 4,215 freshmen, 3,401 sophomores, 1,903 juniors, and 1,757 seniors. One student will randomly be chosen to receive an award. What percent chance is there that it will be a junior?

163

Albert, Bob, and Carl are eating at an all-you-can-eat buffet. Albert makes 2.4 times as many trips to the buffet as Bob, and Bob makes six fewer trips than Carl. What is the smallest possible total number of trips the three makes to the buffet, assuming that each person makes at least one trip?

164

Mia was training for a race by running up and down a hill. It took her sixty minutes to run up the two-mile hill and forty minutes to run down it. How long would it take Mia to run one mile on a flat surface?

165

All of the students at a high school are playing basketball, football, or both. Seventy-three percent of the students are basketball players, and sixty-two percent are football players. If there are 200 students, how many of them are playing both basketball and football?

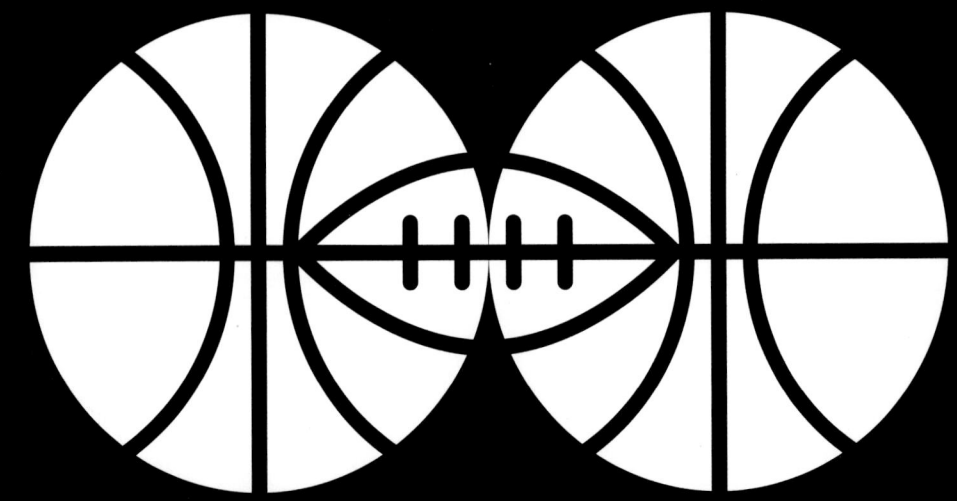

166

Each child in the Smith family has at least three brothers and four sisters. What is the smallest number of children the Smith family might have?

167

Dominic and his sister can build a wall five bricks long and five bricks high in one minute. How long will it take them to build a wall ten bricks long and ten bricks high?

168

Zack and Dennis each have a collection of matchbox cars. Zack says that if Dennis will give him nine cars, they will have an equal number; but if Zack will give Dennis nine of his cars, Dennis will have four times as many cars as Zack. How many matchbox cars does Dennis have?

169

Newport Beach and San Diego are eighty-eight miles apart. If Erica leaves Newport Beach on a bicycle traveling ten miles per hour and Alison leaves San Diego on foot, traveling one mile per hour, how many miles will Erics have to travel before meeting Alison on the way?

170

Sophia spent one-fourth of her life as a girl, one-eighth as a youth, and one-half as an adult. If Joan spent ten years as an old woman, how old is she?

171

At the playground, there are ten bicycles and tricycles. If the total number of wheels is twenty-four, how many tricycles are there?

172

If it takes five dolphins five minutes to eat five fish, how many minutes would it take four dolphins to eat four fish?

173

An upholsterer is putting new fabric on the back of a chair. The size of the fabric is 27 inches × 27 inches. The upholsterer uses tacks all along the edges of the square so that there are twenty-eight tacks on each side of the square. Each tack is the same distance from the neighboring tacks. How many tacks in all does the upholsterer use?

174

There are two flagpoles on the military base. One pole is sixteen-feet tall and casts a shadow four-feet long on the ground. The second flagpole is sixty-four feet tall. How long would the shadow on the second flagpole be?

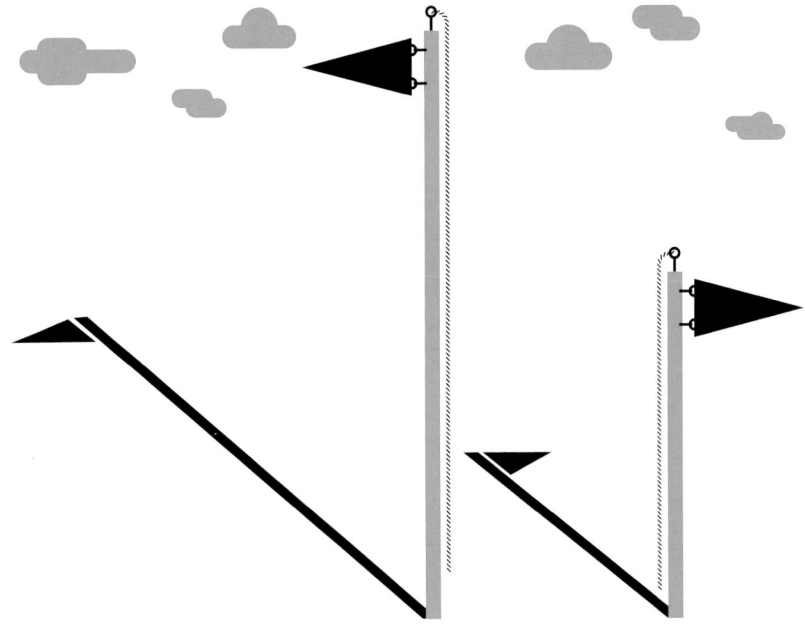

175

Errol, a teacher at the local elementary school, likes to use chalk. He just bought a pack of sixteen sticks. When a stick is three-quarters gone, it gets too small for him to use, so he stops using it. When he has enough of these small pieces to make another stick of the original size, he joins them together and adds them back into the box as a new stick. If Errol uses one piece of chalk each day, how many days would his box of sixteen last?

176

Tim owns a mason company and was hired to build a brick house. The entire house can be built in thirty-one days with five masons. Ten days after they started building the house, Tim hired ten more masons to get the house built quicker. How many more days are required to finish the house?

177

Lucy just finished all four final exams for the semester. She found out that her average score was eighty-one. She also found out that her average in Physics and Math was seventy-eight. What was her average score for English and History?

178

The backgammon world championship took place in Monte Carlo. The tournament was organized in a round-robin format, with every participant playing a match against every other player once. If 105 matches were played in total, how many players were there in the tournament?

179

The family dog, Buster, weighs eighty pounds more than Oscar, the cat. If their combined weight is 120 pounds, how much does Buster weigh?

180

Annika's family sent her to summer camp. In the mornings, she would run and in the evenings she would play softball. She only did one thing each day, however, and there were a few days when she decided to do nothing at all. There were thirteen mornings when she did nothing, eleven evenings when she didn't play softball, and a total of sixteen days when she either ran or played softball. How long was Annika at camp?

181

The local factory's workforce is twenty percent part-time workers, with the rest of the workers full-time. At the end of the year, thirty percent of the full-time workers received bonuses. If seventy-two full-time workers received bonuses, how many workers does the factory employ?

182

Two rival colleges decided on a tug of war. From their starting positions, the University of Minnesota pulls the University of Wisconsin forward three meters, and is then pulled forward themselves five meters. Wisconsin then pulls Minnesota forward two meters. If the first college to be pulled forward ten meters loses, how many more meters must Wisconsin pull Minnesota forward to win?

183

Nate finds that by wearing different combinations of the jackets, shirts, and pairs of pants that he owns, he can create ninety different outfits. If he owns five jackets and three pairs of pants, how many shirts does he own?

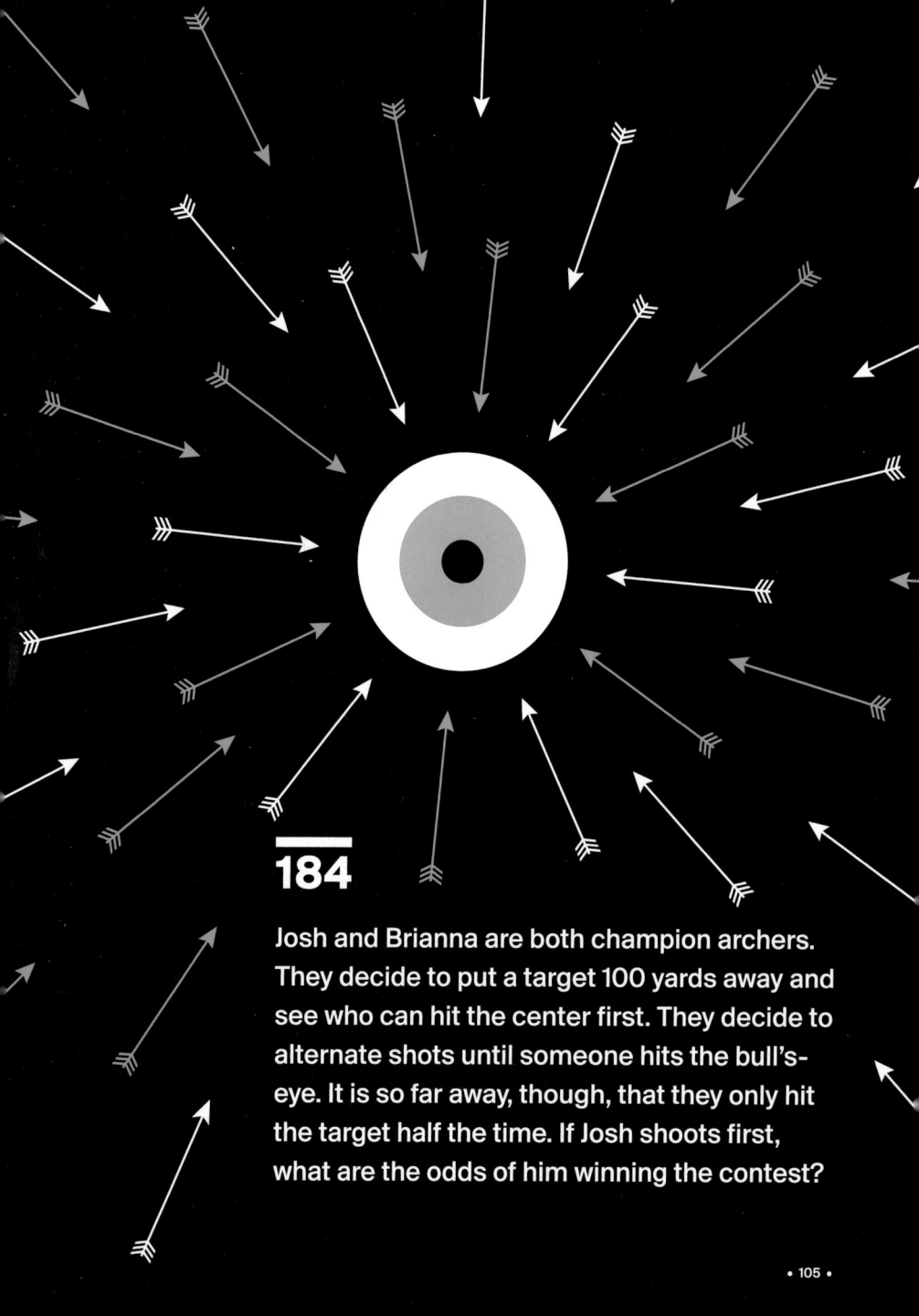

184

Josh and Brianna are both champion archers. They decide to put a target 100 yards away and see who can hit the center first. They decide to alternate shots until someone hits the bull's-eye. It is so far away, though, that they only hit the target half the time. If Josh shoots first, what are the odds of him winning the contest?

185

A fog horn sounds regularly five times a minute. A neighboring fog horn blows regularly four times a minute. If they blow simultaneously, after how many seconds will they blow together again?

186

The Cullinan Diamond is the largest diamond in the world. A group of twelve thieves stole it from the Queen of England. During the getaway, however, they dropped the diamond, and it broke into seven equal pieces. They took the seven pieces to a jeweler and asked him to divide them evenly, so each of the twelve thieves gets an equal amount. How did the jeweler divide the pieces?

187

A ship is sitting in port and the crew hangs a rope ladder over the side so the people can get on and off the ship. If the tide rises one inch per hour, at the end of five hours how much of the ladder will be remaining above water, assuming that ten feet were above water when the tide began to rise?

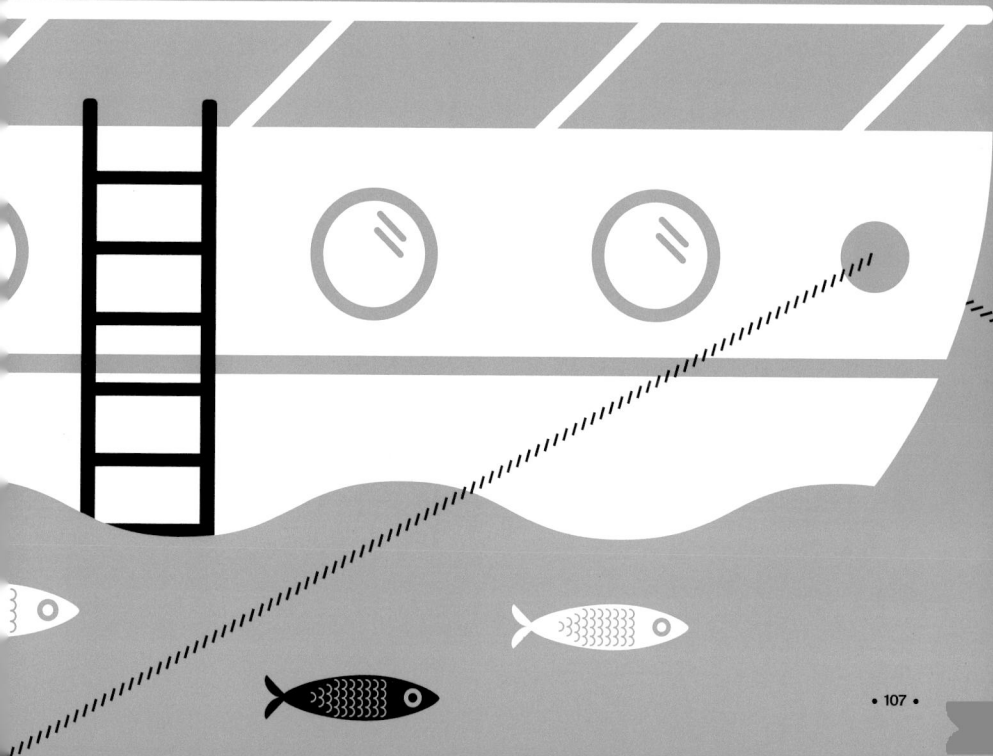

188

If today is Thursday, what is the day that follows the day that comes after the day that precedes the day before yesterday?

189

A man went to an auction and bought a wolf, a goat, and a bag of grain. When he leaves the auction, he starts walking home. To get home, he must cross a river, but he's only allowed to take one item across the bridge with him at a time. If he leaves the wolf with the goat, the wolf will eat the goat. If the goat is left alone with the grain, the goat will eat the grain. How can the man cross the river without any of his possessions being eaten?

190

Alison owes Robert 4.00, Robert owes Christine 3.00, and Carol owes Alison 5.00 If Christine settles all the debts by giving money to both Alison and Robert, how much will she give Alison?

THE SOLUTIONS

01

Peter wins again. Peter is the faster runner and he can run the extra five meters faster than Bill.

02

Billy sold the card twice, for 10.00 and 8.00. He paid 15.00 for the card so he came out ahead by 3.00.

03

Twenty-five lollipops cost 0.25 each. 6.25 equals 625 cents. And 625 divided by 25 = 25.

04

Twelve months. When one person is host, three other people could be the snack provider. Each person gets a chance to be host for three months, each month with a different snack provider. In total, there are twelve different host/snack combinations.

05

It would be more cost effective to get the rust-proofing done. Without the rust-proofing the cost is 17.50 per wheel per year and with the rust-proofing the cost is 16.66 per wheel per year.

06

Adam got there first using his bicycle.

07

They are both making the same amount. Let's say that on their first year they both earn 10,000 In year two, Alison gets a raise to 11,000 and Eric's pay drops to 9,000. In year three, Alison's pay drops by ten percent and goes to 9,900 while Eric's pay rises ten percent and goes from 9,000 to 9,900. They are both now earning 9,900 a year.

08

The first shooter has a two-thirds chance of hitting his opponent first.

09

Beth.

10

Dropping it in the rowboat. Since the marble is denser than water, dropping it into the rowboat will raise the water level higher. Try substituting a marble for a fully-inflated balloon. If you managed to push the balloon underwater it would raise the water level considerably higher than if you dropped the balloon into the rowboat.

11

They played eleven games. John lost three games. He had to win three additional games to break even. Then he had to win five more games to win 50.00. 3 + 3 + 5 = 11

12

Nine times. 1:23, 2:34, 3:45, 4:56, 9:10, 10:11, 11:12, 12:13, 12:34.

13

None. 4 + 8 + 12 + 16 + 20 = 60. Because this total is the exact number of pies sold, there could not have been any pies sold on the first day.

14

Forty jellybeans in the jar.

15

One gold bar weighs five kilograms. By removing one gold bar from each side of the scale, two gold bars weigh ten kilograms total.

16

Steve must give Lisa five marbles. He would then have five less, she would have five more for a difference of ten.

17

Six.

18

The only matching colors available for Louisa's present is red paper and a red bow. The only contrasting paper color remaining for Samantha's present is silver. Maria's present is left with green paper and a gold bow.

19

Cut four of the apples into three pieces each, and then cut the three remaining apples into four pieces each.

20

Twenty-nine days. The doubling still occurs each day; we can just rule out the first day since it was doubled initially.

21

Three sons and four daughters.

22

One hour and five minutes.

23

Seven. Jess has none and Courtney has one.

24

She started with 100.00.

25

One. Consider jar #1. Overall possible permutations (N=9!), there is a one-in-nine chance that this jar gets its correct label. Same result concerning each of the eight jars #2, 3, 4,...9. In total, there are 9 × N/9 = N jars correctly labeled; that means (N-correctly-labeled-jars/(N-possible-configurations) = 1 jar is labeled correctly on average.

26

Ninety-nine. With only one winner, there must be ninety-nine losers, requiring ninety-nine matches.

27

Twenty cents.

28

The weight will rise.

29

Seven. To average two hours a day over six days, Olivia must practice 2 × 6, or twelve hours. From Monday through Friday, she practices five hours—one hour each day. To total twelve hours, she must practice 12–5, or seven hours, on Saturday.

30

160.00 dollars. The easy way to solve this is to divide 320 in half, since the half of the seventy-nine percent that tipped two dollars is the same as the full seventeen percent tipping one dollar.

31

Amelia has three handbags, one gold, one brown, and one white.

32

Twelve jellybeans. Ava ate half the remaining jellybeans plus three more to leave none, so she must have eaten six jellybeans. George ate half the jellybeans and left six, meaning there were twelve to start.

33

Five cars. 1,500 × 5 = 7,500 profit.

34

Ten games. Craig won the first three, and Dan had to win the next seven in order to win $4.

35

John is the tallest, then Bill, then Mick.

36

Mia is eight years older than Emily.

37

She lost 100.00.

38

Enriqué is sleeping between Ricardo and Juan.

39

116.00.

40

Tobias made each person ride another person's horse. This would ensure that everyone would want to come in first so they wouldn't lose.

41

It only passes ten times.

42

Yes. She has seven daughters.

43

Muhammad started with 62.00.

44

Eleven. Trains pass by every half hour for nine total, plus two pulling into the cities.

45

Thirty-one runners total. Since the track is a closed circuit, we simply add $\frac{1}{5} + \frac{5}{6} = 31/30$. 30 runners plus Oscar.

46

Ten kids.

47

France.

48

Eleven tires total. 4,000 kilometers × 4 tires = 16,000 total kilometers. 1,500 × 11 = 16,500 total kilometers.

49

Six pairs. Five pairs will only get her fifty miles and both marathons are fifty-two miles.

50

Total cost of meal is 60.00. 3 people × 20.00 = 60.00. Eight dishes have been eaten, therefore each dish costs 7.50. Blake brought 5 dishes × 7.50 = 37.50 minus his 20.00 share or 17.50. Brian brought 3 dishes × 7.50 minus his share = 2.50.

51

Eight chickens and fourteen goats.

52

Twenty-seven rungs.

53

She should take the first job. In two years, it will have paid 56,000, while the second job will have paid only 55,000.

54

They must charge 4.00 per serving to make a 100 percent profit.

55

Erik can reach the summit using only two Sherpas. The three of them leave base camp, each with four days' worth of food. At the end of the first day, they all have three days' worth of food left. The first Sherpa leaves two days' worth of food with Erik and the other Sherpa, and heads back to base camp with one days' worth of food in his pack. On the second day, the last Sherpa heads back to base camp after leaving one days' worth of food with Erik. Erik now has four days' worth of food and only four days left to get to the summit. He will die of starvation on the way down, however.

56

Fifty-nine cents. Ten seven-cent coins minus the eleven-cent coin.

57

Ten 1.00 bills, one hundred 50.00 bills, nine 10.00 bills, and eighteen 50.00 bills.

58

Her average speed is 6.7 miles per hour. It takes Elena two hours to run the first ten miles and one hour to run the last ten miles, meaning she needs three hours to run the total of twenty miles.

59

Label the sacks from 1 to 5. Take one coin out of sack 1, and label it 1. Take two coins out of sack 2, and label them both with a 2. Take three coins out of sack 3, and label each with a 3. Continue this pattern with sacks 4 and 5. Put these fifteen coins on the tray of the scale. If all fifteen weighed one pound, the scale would register fifteen pounds, but since one or more of the coins weighs only nine-tenths of a pound, the scale will register less than fifteen. Subtract the number on the scale from fifteen. Your answer will tell you the number of the sack with the lighter coins. (If the scale registers 14.8 pounds, it's sack 2. If the scale registers 14.5 pounds, it's sack 5.)

60

Bernie had the best average. Derek batted 73.3 percent, and Bernie batted 75 percent.

61

Ten blocks.

62

They both drank the same amount of caffeine.

63

Alison has one cat and one goldfish.

64

The time is 8:30.

65

You still only need seventeen bakers.

66

There are four possibilities:
One spoon and one fork.
Two spoons.
One fork and one spoon.
Two forks.
In three of the four possibilities, you'll wind up with at least one spoon. So the chances of picking at least one spoon are three in four or, in another phrasing, three to one.

67

If you add up all the losses, you find that 100 students lost a total of 310 items. That total means that, at a minimum, 100 students lost three items, and ten (the remainder when dividing 310 by 100) must have lost all four items.

68

Coco, Rocky, Winston, Fluffy, and Lulu.

69

Ten cookies.

70

Amelia had 6.00 before she found the 4.00.

71

Eight days. The snail makes one foot of progress every twenty-four hours. So after seven days, she will have climbed seven feet. Then on day eight, she will climb the three feet she manages per day and gets out of the well.

72

420 students: This is the only number under 500 that can be divided evenly by 3, 4, 5, and 7.

73

Beth is twenty-two years old.

74

Four flies (twenty-four legs) and three spiders (twenty-four legs). No other combination will work.

75

Andy has gone through eight times, Bill four times, Chris eleven times, Drake six times, Eric three times.

76

From youngest to oldest, the six brothers are ten, fourteen, eighteen, twenty-two, twenty-six, and thirty.

77

Four people can make twelve hats in six hours.

78

Five pieces of candy at 0.10, one piece of candy at 0.03, ninety-four pieces of candy at 2 pieces for 0.01 equals 1.00.

79

Bill took eleven lessons.

80

Six shoes. If he takes out five shoes, he could have one of each color, with no two matching colors.

81

John spent 2,500 and 4,500 for a total of 7,000. John sold the painting for 3,500 and 5,500 for a total of 9,000. John came out ahead by 2,000.

82

260. Sophia makes 280. If Liam makes 50.00 more than this, then Liam must make 280 + 50.00 or 330. Dan makes 70.00 less than this amount, or 260.

83

Juanita solved eighteen puzzles correctly, earning thirty-six points. She failed to solve twelve correctly, losing thirty-six points.

84

The rain gauge was half-filled on Saturday. It doubled on Sunday, to become completely filled.

85

33.3 percent. If the car originally cost 30,000, with the twenty-five percent deduction, it would cost 22,500. To bring the price back to the original 30,000, you'd have to add 7,500, which is one-third of 22,500, or 33.3 percent.

86

He should buy the ring from the first jewelry store. Hypothetically, if Brian proposed twice, Andrea should say yes once and no once. This would mean that if he bought the ring from the first store twice he would have spent 6,600 and if he bought the ring from the second store twice he would have spent 7,000. On average, the ring would cost him 3,300 from the first store and 3,500 from the second one.

87

The Spanish diplomat would get assassinated 5 times (50% × 10) and the French diplomat would get assassinated 1.5 times (25% × 6). Therefore, the Spanish diplomat is in greater danger.

88

Seven rows. eight oranges in the bottom row, two in the top.

89

Sixty feet.

90

There are four players on each team.

91

Four hours.

92

The five football players will win. If there were only four football players on one side and two soccer players on the other side, it would be a tie.

93

Eighty miles.

94

Ralph. Tommy is selling the shoes for 63.75 and Ralph is selling them for 63.00.

95
Charlotte picked fifteen.

96
Container E holds the apple juice. The second customer can buy twice as much as the first customer if the first customer buys Containers A and C (for a total of sixty-six quarts) and the second customer buys Containers B, D, and F (for a total of 132 quarts). The remaining container, E, must hold the apple juice.

97
Ninety-nine seconds. Each cut, including the 99th, produces two pieces of wire.

98
Trent makes 24.00, Mary makes 48.00, Shawn makes 72.00.

99
Forty-five eggs.

100
Fill the three-liter jug and pour it into the five-liter jug. Fill the three-liter jug again and add the water to the same five-liter jug, filling it to the top. What's left in the three-liter jug is one liter of water.

101
Twenty-two years old.

102
36.00.

103
Georgia slept through half the trip.

104
She drives 200 miles on the last day. If n = miles traveled in one day, let each subsequent day be n + 20 (the daily increase in miles). With this you'll find that she would have to have traveled forty miles the first day, sixty the second day, 100 on the fourth day, and 200 on the ninth and final day. This is the only way it would add up to 1080.

105
They've been playing for 720 weeks or 13.8 years. The number of possible seating arrangements is $6 \times 5 \times 4 \times 3 \times 2$, which is 720.

106
1,000 divided by 175.00 is 5.7, so they worked on the roof for six days.

107
Twenty-four additional gold rings.

108
Twenty-seven gumballs.

109

The grouper weighs 102 pounds. The weight of the halibut is given indirectly by saying two halibut weigh the same as one swordfish. One grouper and two halibut are equal to the weight of one sturgeon and one halibut. One grouper and one halibut must have the same weight as one sturgeon. So, the grouper is 120 pounds minus eighteen pounds, or 102 pounds.

110

Charlie has twenty-one minutes and forty-nine seconds.

111

Use two cuts to make an X so that you have four pieces, then make a horizontal cut through the cake to make eight pieces.

112

Yes.
XXO
XOX
OXX

113

Twenty-five cows would eat all the grass in five days.

114

One jumbo stapler, twenty-nine regular staplers, and seventy tiny staplers.

115

75.00.

116

Forty-three nails.

117

Two-thirds.

118

Flip both hourglasses over. When the four-minute hourglass runs out, flip it back over immediately. When the seven-minute hourglass runs out, flip that back over immediately, too. One minute later, the four-minute hourglass will run out again. At this point, flip the seven-minute hourglass back over. The seven-minute hourglass has only been running for a minute, so when it is flipped over again it will only run for a minute more before running out. When it does, exactly nine minutes will have passed.

119

Bill had forty-nine watches and Mick had thirty-five.

120

62.5 peanuts.

121

Dragonlady won, Atomic Angie came in second, and Quick Ted came in third.

122

Two half-full barrels are dumped into one of the empty barrels. Two more half-full barrels are dumped into another one of the empty barrels. This results in nine full barrels, three half-full barrels, and nine empty barrels. Each son gets three full barrels, one half-full barrel, and three empty barrels.

123

Take a piece of fruit from the box marked "cherries and strawberries." If the fruit you take is a cherry, then that box must be the box containing just cherries. Therefore, the box marked "strawberries" can't be the box containing just cherries, and it can't be the box containing just strawberries either, so it must be the box containing cherries and strawberries. The remaining box is therefore the box containing just strawberries.

124

Ask one of the men what the other man would answer to the question, "Is the door on the left the correct door?" Then assume the answer you are given is false and act on that knowledge. If the man you ask is the liar, he'll incorrectly give you the truthful man's answer. If the man you ask is the truthful man, he'll correctly give you the liar's wrong answer.

125

Say It Fast came in first. Lion Heart and Sir Oscar tied for second place. Silver Wagon came in fourth. Master David came in fifth.

126

Five yellow birds were seen.

127

Darren had his own coat, Tom's hat, Rob's gloves, and Matt's cane. Tom had his own coat, Matt's hat, Darren's gloves, and Rob's cane. Rob had Matt's coat, his own hat, Tom's gloves, and Darren's cane. Matt had Rob's coat, Darren's hat, his own gloves, and Tom's cane.

128

Light one fuse at both ends and, at the same time, light the second fuse at one end. When the first fuse has completely burned, a half hour has elapsed and the second fuse has a half hour left to go. At this time, light the second fuse from the other end. This will cause it to burn out in fifteen more minutes. At that point, exactly forty-five minutes will have elapsed.

129

Three-quarters.

130

Seventeen. You just need to find two numbers, seven apart, that add up to 27. With trial and error you should be able to find them soon—ten and seventeen; there must be seventeen women working at the office.

131

Ingrid spent 22.00.
The headphones cost 14.00.
The protective case costs 5.00.
And the screen protector costs 3.00.

132

20.00.

133

Camera: 52.25.
Ruler: 0.50.
Ice cream bar: 0.25.

134

Sixteen. Find the total number of gumballs in the bag, then divide by the new number of children who will be sharing them.

135

Eighteen stations. The subway will pass 60/10 or six times as many stations in one hour as it passes in ten minutes. In ten minutes, it passes three stations; in sixty minutes, it must pass 6 × 3, or eighteen stations.

136

You can learn the contents of all three boxes by drawing just one marble. The key to the solution is your knowledge that the labels on all three of the boxes are incorrect. You must draw a marble from the box labeled "black-white." Assume that the marble drawn is black. You know then that the other marble in this box must be black also, otherwise the label would be correct. Since you have now identified the box containing two black marbles, you can at once tell the contents of the box marked "white-white." you know it cannot contain two white marbles, because its label has to be wrong; it cannot contain two black marbles, because you have identified that box; therefore, it must contain one black and one white marble. The third box, of course, must then be the one holding two white marbles. You can solve the puzzle by the same reasoning if the marble you draw from the "black-white" box happens to be white instead of black.

137

You buy one cow, nine pigs, and ninety chickens.

138

IBM is at 70 and Microsoft is at 105⅜.

139

Fifty percent.

140
27.00.

141
During his five turns at the billiards table he sank eight, fourteen, twenty, twenty-six, and thirty-two balls.

142
There were twenty-six men and twenty women, or forty-six altogether at the club.

143
The balloon is 200 meters above the lake.

144
It will take the train eighteen minutes. The front of the train has to initially travel ten kilometers to leave the tunnel, and then a further one-half kilometer until the rear of the train has left the tunnel—a total of ten and one-half kilometers. Which takes $60 \times (10.5 / 35) = 18$ minutes.

145
Seven members and seven committees.

146
The price of the TV is less than it was before the twenty-five percent increase and the twenty-five percent decrease. If the TV cost 1,000.00, you know that twenty-five percent of 1,000 is 250. So, after the twenty-five percent increase, the cost was 1,250. Now find twenty-five percent of 1,250. Subtract this amount (312.50) from 1,250.to find the reduced price. It's 937.50—that's 62.50 less than the original price of 1,000.

147
FedEx should charge 4,000 for a large truckload. Since each dimension of the large truck (height, width, and length) is twice that of the small truck, the volume of the large truck is eight times that of the small truck. So, for a large truckload, FedEx should charge eight times the price of a small truckload. That's 8×500.00, or 4,000.

148
Anne has $\frac{8}{35}$ and Ken has $\frac{6}{35}$.

149
Twenty-one percent. $64 + 22 - 7 = 79$. $100 - 79$ is 21.

150
None.

151
There can only be one brown-haired contestant; therefore, the other ninety-nine have blonde hair..

152
It weighs half a pound. $\frac{1}{5} \times \frac{5}{2} = \frac{5}{10}$ or half a pound.

153
One and seven-eighths hours.

154
Forty-five.

155
195.

156
325.00 per delivery.

157
One minute. Remember, they double every minute, so when the dish is half full, it will only take one more doubling to fill it.

158
Twenty-four.

159
Fifty.

160
Eight throws.

161
Six. Danielle made five cigarettes from the twenty-five butts, smoked them, and then made an additional cigarette from the five butts that were left from the five that she made.

162
Seventeen percent. Divide the number of juniors (1,903) by the total number of students (11,276).

163
There were twenty-eight total trips made, with Albert making twelve of them, Bob making five, and Carl making eleven.

164
Mia can run one mile on a flat surface in twenty-four minutes. She can run three miles an hour downhill and two miles an hour uphill. If you take the average of the two rates, you find that Mia runs 2.5 miles per hour on a flat surface.

165
Thirty-five percent are playing both for a total of seventy students.

166
The smallest number of children the Smith family might have is nine.

167
Four minutes. The first wall has twenty-five bricks. The second wall has four times as many, so it will take four times as long, or four minutes.

168
Dennis has thirty-nine cars.

169

Together they cover the distance at eleven miles per hour so they will cover the distance of eighty-eight miles in eight hours. In eight hours they will meet and Erica will have traveled eighty miles.

170

Sophia is eighty years old.

171

There are four tricycles in the park.

172

It would still take five minutes for four dolphins to eat four fish.

173

108 tacks. The four corners of the square have one tack each, so each side of the square now requires twenty-six tacks. The total number of tacks used = $4 + (4 \times 26) = 108$.

174

Sixteen feet. $(64 / 16) \times 4 = 16$ feet.

175

Twenty-one days. Errol has sixteen pieces in the original box. The small pieces make four new pieces and the small pieces of the four new pieces make one more for twenty-one.

176

Seven days will finish the house.

177

Eighty-four was the average.
Total marks in 4 exams = $4 \times 81 = 324$.
Total marks for Physics and Math = $2 \times 78 = 156$.
Total marks in English and History = $324 - 156 = 168$.
Average marks in English and History= $168/2 = 84$.

178

There are fifteen players in the tournament. $14 + 13 + ... + 2 + 1 = 105$.

179

Buster weighs 100 pounds.

180

Annika was at camp for nineteen days.

181

300. Twenty percent of the workers are part-time, so eighty percent of the workers are full-time. Thirty percent received bonuses and this amounted to seventy-two workers. Thirty percent of eighty percent of total workers (n) equals seventy-two. $3/10 \times 8/10 \times n = 72$, or $24/100 \times n = 72$.
Therefore, $n = 72 \times 100/24$ or 300.

182

Six. Find out how far the University of Minnesota has moved thus far. They pulled the University of Wisconsin forward three meters, so Minnesota moved backward three meters. Then they were pulled forward five meters and then a further two meters. In total then they have moved forward $(-3) + 5 + 2 = 4$ meters. They must be pulled a further six meters to be pulled ten meters forward.

183

Six. For every pair of pants, Nate can wear five different jackets, giving five different combinations for each pair of pants, or $3 \times 15 = 15$ different combinations of pants and jackets. With each of these combinations he can wear any of his different shirts. The different combinations of shirts, jackets, and pants is (number of shirts) / 15. We are told this equals ninety, so ninety divided by fifteen equals six.

184

Josh has a two-thirds chance of successfully hitting the bull's-eye before Brianna does.

185

Sixty. If you convert everything to seconds, the first fog horn blows every twelve seconds and the second fog horn blows every fifteen seconds.

Then find the lowest common denominator, which is sixty, and you arrive at the answer.

186

The jeweler cut four of the pieces into three pieces each and then cut the three remaining pieces into four pieces each, and divided them accordingly.

187

Ten feet. The ship will rise with the tide and so will the ladder, so it won't affect the amount that is above water.

188

Wednesday.

189

Take the goat across and leave it on the other side. Then go back, get the wolf. Bring the wolf to the other side and take the goat back with you. Take the grain to the other side and leave it there, then go back and get the goat.

190

1.00. Christine is owed 3.00 by Robert, and she owes 5.00 to Alison. She needs a cash loss of 2.00 to settle all debts. Alison, on the other hand, is owed 5.00 by Christine and owes 4.00 to Robert. She must have a gain of 1.00. Since Christine settles all debts, this 1.00 must come from Christine, and this is the answer.

ABOUT THE AUTHOR

Nathan Haselbauer was the president and founder of the International High IQ Society and helped write theTest for Exceptional Intelligence, one of the most difficult and popular high-ceiling intelligence tests available.

**ALSO AVAILABLE
FROM FAIR WINDS PRESS**

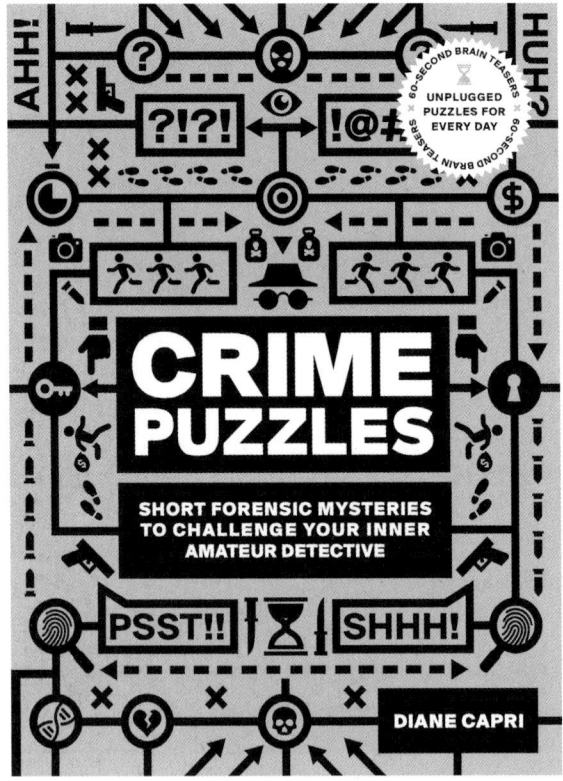

60-Second Brain Teasers Crime Puzzles
978-1-59233-979-2